FIT
TO
FLY

✈ **Exercises** ✈ **Relaxation** ✈ **Health** ✈ **Q & A**

Dr Wayne Sapsford

NEW
HOLLAND

First published in 2004 by New Holland Publishers (UK) Ltd
London • Cape Town • Sydney • Auckland

10 9 8 7 6 5 4 3 2 1

www.newhollandpublishers.com

Garfield House, 86–88 Edgware Road, London W2 2EA, UK

80 McKenzie Street, Cape Town 8001, South Africa

14 Aquatic Drive, Frenchs Forest, NSW 2086, Australia

218 Lake Road, Northcote, Auckland, New Zealand

ISBN 1 84330 564 X

Publishing Manager: Jo Hemmings
Senior Editor: Kate Michell
Assistant Editor: Rose Hudson
Design & Cover design: Gülen Shevki
Production: Lucy Hulme
Illustrator: Juliet Percival
Index: Dorothy Frame

Reproduction by Pica Digital Pte Ltd, Singapore
Printed and bound by Times Offset (M) Sdn. Bhd., Malaysia

Publisher's Note:
While every care has been taken in the preparation of this book, readers are advised to seek
professional advice if in any doubt about their health. Neither the author nor publisher may be held
responsible for any claim or action resulting from the use of this book or the information it contains.

CONTENTS ✈

INTRODUCTION

The dramatic increase in commercial passenger air travel in the last quarter of a century is unprecedented. Cheap flights and wide-bodied aircraft with flexible seating options have made flying accessible to all. It is estimated that over 1.5 billion people fly each year and that this is likely to double in the next 10 years. There are over 40,000 flights per day around the world and at any one time there are some 13 million passengers in the air. Planes fly longer distances, spend more time in the air and do so at greater altitudes than ever before. The future holds yet larger aircraft, longer flying hours and more people being transported to more distant destinations.

Since the birth of aviation medicine, doctors and scientists have concentrated mainly on the flight-deck crew, flight attendants and ground-support personnel. Recently, however, issues of passenger health, safety and comfort have come under the spotlight, as media attention has highlighted concerns in these areas. Deep vein thrombosis (DVT), cabin air quality, infection, cosmic radiation and jet lag are the principal health issues that have been identified as needing more research, and they are now being intensely investigated.

This book explains the unique environment that we, as passengers, experience during a typical flight, and how it relates to and can impact on our health. The phases of a typical flight are explained so that you can fly with increased confidence, knowing a little more about what is happening and why. There are sections on how to prepare yourself properly for a flight and what to do to stay healthy on the aircraft and immediately after disembarkation. Specific medical problems, such as travellers' thrombosis (DVT), transmission of infection, cosmic radiation, jet lag and others, are dealt with in more detail, and methods are given by which you can help combat the deleterious effects of flying on your body. There are also chapters covering other flying issues, including fear of flying, and frequently asked questions about aircraft in general.

By gaining a better understanding of the potential problems of flying and how to minimize their impact on your health, you will be better able to make informed choices in order to keep fit and healthy in the skies; in short, to ensure that you are 'fit to fly'.

FLYING ENVIRONMENTS

Intercontinental air travel by modern commercial passenger jet is a wonderful experience, only made possible by advances in technology in the past 50 years. It is, however, a very different experience for the human body than travelling long distances by modern passenger train. During a long train journey you are travelling at speed in a metal tube for five or more hours, relatively cramped, often bored or trying to sleep or work, or even looking out over the countryside. When cruising in a passenger jet, on the other hand, you are at an altitude of 30–40,000 feet above the Earth. The environment inside this speeding metal tube is very different from that found in a train at sea level. It is the altitude that is directly or indirectly responsible for all the additional potential problems associated with passenger flying.

It will, therefore, be helpful to understand a little about the atmosphere on the other side of the window through which you stare as you survey the world from your aircraft seat. It is also useful to know something about the cabin environment you are sitting in, and how the aircraft insulates you from that unfriendly place outside: the upper troposphere or lower stratosphere.

The troposphere and the stratosphere
The troposphere is part of the atmosphere that surrounds the Earth, held there by the pull of gravity. It exists above the surface of the Earth and contains the air we breathe and the weather. The tropopause forms the roof of the troposphere and the floor of the stratosphere, beyond which is space. Depending on where over the surface of the Earth you are, the altitude of the tropopause varies between about 26,000 feet at the poles and approximately 58,000 feet at the equator.

Passenger jets use the thin, cloudless air in the upper troposphere, the tropopause and stratosphere above it, to allow them to fly at their maximum speeds while being at their most fuel-efficient. The tropopause is well above the weather, which is responsible for most of the turbulence experienced in a flight. Typically, a long-haul passenger jet will cruise at about 550 miles per hour relative to the ground and at about 39,000 feet above sea level, that is, over seven miles high.

The atmosphere at this altitude is very different to that on the Earth's surface. Atmospheric pressure and air density are less than one quarter of that at the Earth's surface, and any given quantity of gas will expand to more than four times its sea-level volume (see page 10). The temperature outside is about 56°C below freezing. Although the proportion of the essential life-giving gas, oxygen, in the air is still 21

Position of cruising aircraft within Earth's atmosphere

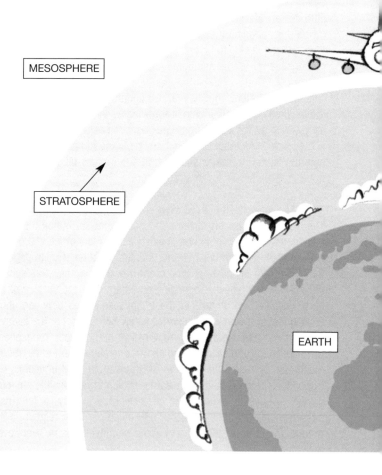

MESOSPHERE

STRATOSPHERE

EARTH

per cent (the same proportion to that we breathe at the surface of the Earth), because of the nature of gases and the process of breathing, the pressure of the oxygen in the air at 39,000 feet is insufficient to sustain human life. You would lose consciousness in under one minute in that environment. Additional oxygen is required at altitudes above 10,000 feet, and 100 per cent oxygen is needed above 33,000 feet.

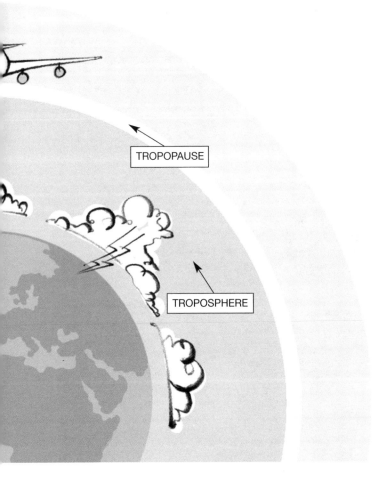

TROPOPAUSE

TROPOSPHERE

Inside the aircraft cabin

The atmosphere inside the aircraft cabin is not identical to that on the Earth's surface. Although not obvious to all passengers, cabin air pressure is lower than on Earth at sea level, so air in the cabin is less dense. You may have detected the pressure changing on the climb or descent by your ears 'popping', when you feel the need to equalize pressures between the cabin and your ears by swallowing, moving your

The Valsalva manoeuvre

With the back of your mouth closed, pinch your nose and blow out, straining a little to cause the ears to pop.

jaw or by employing the Valsalva manoeuvre: blowing out against your pinched nose with the back of your mouth (glottis) closed – see opposite. At cruising altitudes the air inside the aircraft cabin is pressurized to a similar level to that found 6–8,000 feet up a mountain. Within such a pressurized aircraft, additional oxygen is not required, even at altitudes of over 39,000 feet. However, every safety briefing tells passengers how to use the 100 per cent oxygen supply that automatically drops from the overhead panel in the event of a sudden cabin depressurization.

In passenger jets, pressurization is achieved by taking and compressing outside air from the engine, cooling it, and conducting it through non-return valves into the cabin. The flow is controlled to give sufficient movement of air through the cabin. The air escapes via discharge valves, which are controlled to maintain the pressure difference between the cabin and the outside. There is, therefore, no danger of the air supply running out (see diagram on pages 52–3).

The oxygen in the aircraft at 39,000 feet is thus maintained at a level compatible with normal human activities, although it is significantly lower than on Earth at sea level. Although 21 per cent of the cabin air is oxygen, the reduced pressure makes it equivalent to breathing only 16–17 per cent oxygen at sea level. The saturation of red blood cells with oxygen, normally 97–100 per cent in healthy people at sea level, reduces to 90–93 per cent at a cabin pressure of 6,000 feet. This reduction in saturation is not noticed in the healthy person but may be significant for those with some types of cardiac or respiratory disease or with anaemia.

The change in pressure within the aircraft cabin on the initial climb and, more significantly, during the descent causes gases to expand and contract. Any gas trapped in the body, for example, in the middle ear, the sinuses or the gut, will expand by 20–30 per cent on the climb from take-off to the cruise. It is normally easy for this expanded gas to escape and this is detected by the sensation of ear 'popping' or passing wind. A poor tooth filling or dental abscess, trapping air generated by infection in a cavity, can cause the tooth to become painful during the climb – aerodontalgia – and abdominal discomfort may be experienced. On the descent to land, the increasing pressure in the aircraft cabin will try to force its way back into the rigid, air-filled cavities, especially the middle ear and sinuses. Equalization of the pressures in the middle ear can usually be achieved by swallowing,

Oxygen levels, temperature and humidity

OUTSIDE AT CRUISING ALTITUDE
Effective available oxygen: 0%
Arterial blood oxygen saturation:
incompatible with life
Temperature: -56°C
Humidity: 0%

**AIRCRAFT CABIN AT
CRUISING ALTITUDE**
Effective available oxygen: 17%
Arterial blood oxygen saturation:
90–93%
Temperature: approximately 20°C
Humidity: 5–20%

EARTH AT SEA LEVEL
Effective available
oxygen: 21%
Arterial blood oxygen
saturation: 97–100%
Temperature:
approximately 15°C
Humidity: 50–75%

moving the jaw or employing the Valsalva manoeuvre (see page 8).

If your ear passages, the Eustachian tubes (which connect the middle ear with the back of the mouth) and sinus foramina (which connect the sinuses with the nose) are blocked by a cold then the gases will not equalize. A pressure difference across the eardrum stretches it and causes earache and partial deafness. You might then experience discomfort or even quite intense pain, as well as partial deafness, during the descent to land. Sinuses can also become exquisitely painful during this phase of flight.

The thin air you breathe in the cabin is potentially dehydrating. Although it is conditioned, the moisture content of cabin air is very low, down to a level of about 5 per cent humidity, lower than most deserts; normal air humidity is between 50 and 75 per cent. Every breath we exhale contains gas and water vapour. As air pressure decreases, water vapour forms an ever greater proportion of each exhaled breath, increasing the water loss from our bodies compared to that which happens at sea level. It is no surprise, then, that you feel very dry after a long flight. This sensation of dryness is mainly a result of the drying of the skin and the mucous membranes in the nose and mouth, and can be improved by the use of a lip balm and moisturizers, as well by being sure to drink enough water throughout the flight and limiting the consumption of alcohol and caffeine-containing substances.

So, the cabin environment, with its less than normal sea level pressure and very dry conditions, is not an ideal place for you to spend prolonged periods of time. It would, however, be prohibitively expensive to pressurize commercial aircraft to sea-level pressure because of the weight and strength that would be required in the aircraft hull to withstand the pressure difference between the interior and the atmosphere outside. Nevertheless, the cabin environment in passenger aircraft is well oxygenated and warm compared to the environment on the other side of the window as you look out into the troposphere and stratosphere.

Armed with this information about the troposphere, tropopause and stratosphere and the difference between it and the cabin environment, it is time to consider what is happening, and why, during all the stages of a typical flight. A better understanding of these phases will help allay the anxiety brought about by fear of the unknown.

FLYING STAGES

THE SEVEN STAGES OF FLIGHT

✈ The pre-take-off checks and the taxi

✈ The take-off

✈ The climb

✈ The cruise

✈ The descent

✈ The approach

✈ The landing

✈ An additional potential stage, not normally included in the above set stages, is the go-around (this is embarked on if there is any abnormality during the final approach rather than risk a potentially dangerous landing)

For many people flying is a stressful experience. Stress may manifest itself as anything from an easy-to-contain, mild anxiety during periods of turbulence to a panic attack at the thought of having to take a flight. There is a chapter for truly nervous fliers later in this book (see pages 67–74), but for those who are merely concerned, one of the reasons for your concern is probably that you have no control over your situation, which is exacerbated by lack of knowledge about what is happening during the various phases of your flight.

So that you can better understand what is happening, there follows a brief description of the seven stages of flight.

The pre-take-off checks and the taxi

Once all the passengers are aboard, all the luggage corresponding to the passenger list is loaded and the aircraft is technically ready, then the load sheet can be handed out to the handling agent and the doors will be closed. If passengers are late to board, the aircraft might miss its scheduled departure 'slot' time (a window of only 15 minutes). The flight crew then have to apply for a new, later slot and the aircraft will be delayed. Worse still, if a passenger does not turn up for boarding, becomes ill before boarding or becomes ill on board before take-off and must disembark, or luggage has been loaded that does not belong

to any of the passengers aboard, then the relevant luggage must be removed. No passenger aircraft is allowed to take off with luggage on board belonging to a non-boarded passenger.

During embarkation you may hear and feel the clunks and occasional jolts as the pallets of luggage are manoeuvred into the hold and secured into position. You may also hear and feel the whirrings of motors and clunks as the hold doors are opened and closed.

If there is a delay due, for example, to a missed slot time, the doors are not normally reopened and you are not allowed off the aircraft because a new slot time might become available at short notice. If the delay is going to be greater than 30 minutes and cabin air conditioning cannot be made available, then consideration will be given to disembarkation, in which case it will be necessary to complete all the boarding checks again.

The flight crew complete the pre-take-off checks while at the stand. When you hear the command to 'set the doors to automatic' or 'arm the doors and cross check', the aircraft is set to go. Flight attendants, in pairs, arm the doors, one attendant to each door on either side of the aircraft (the doors are usually in pairs). To arm the doors means to set them to deploy the escape slides/rafts automatically if opened. To cross check is to make sure that the flight attendant opposite has correctly armed his or her door. The doors will now be opened only in an emergency. Once the doors have been armed and cross checked the flight crew is informed and the flight preparations continue.

Once permission is given to leave the stand, you might feel the aircraft being gently pushed back by a small vehicle and/or hear the engines being started. After the engines have been started, the flight crew complete the after-start checks and the aircraft will move forward for the first time. When the engines start you will also notice the air-conditioning system kick into life because it takes its power from the engines rather than from the ground power source or the auxiliary power unit you may have heard whining when you boarded. You are then asked to put your seat belts on, ensure your seat backs are in the upright position and that your tray tables are folded away. Once every passenger has complied with these essential instructions and the flight attendants have checked and counted each passenger, the flight crew will be informed that the cabin is secure. The captain cannot take off before this is confirmed. Like most of the instructions you receive, these are regulations set down in aviation law for your own safety; they are non-negotiable. Failure to comply will delay departure.

Taxiing time varies depending on the distance to the start of the runway, the wind direction and the length of the queue of other aircraft waiting to take off. The flight crew complete the take-off checks during this time, one of which is to ensure the cabin is secure for take-off. The whirrings and hummings you hear are the wings being reconfigured – by lowering the flaps and the leading-edge slats – by the flight crew in preparation for take-off. The captain might be told to hold just short of the runway because landing aircraft have priority.

The take-off

When all the checks are complete, the flight crew will radio that the aircraft is 'ready for departure'. They may then be given clearance for immediate take-off by air traffic control, in which case the aircraft will turn onto the runway and begin its take-off roll in one movement. Otherwise they will be told to 'line up' on the runway and await clearance, after which the take-off roll will begin. At take-off, the engines are set to take-off power and the roll down the runway begins. The engine noise, the acceleration and the bumps in the runway are clearly sensed. Initially the captain steers the aircraft with the nose wheel until the airspeed increases and the rudder becomes effective. You might feel the aircraft sway slightly as the captain maintains a straight line along the runway.

In any commercial jet there are important calculated milestones to be attained during this roll. Typically, the first significant point is at 80 knots (about 92mph). Up to this speed, if there is even the slightest malfunction warning, indicated by either an orange or a red warning light on the flight deck instrument panels, take-off will be aborted and the aircraft will be stopped on the runway. Between this speed and the next milestone, V_1, the aircraft can still be stopped in the event of an emergency, indicated by a red warning light.

The most important milestone is V_1, the speed at or above which the aircraft must take off because there is no longer enough runway to stop the aircraft even in the event of an emergency. Fortunately, even in the event of an engine failure in a twin-engined jet, there is enough power in a single engine to continue the take-off and maintain a safe climb-out speed with a safety margin too. Full power in the remaining

engine is engaged. The captain and first officer regularly practise this emergency procedure at every single simulator check.

V$_{rotate}$ is the next milestone and the nose wheel will lift off the runway. As the aircraft rotates and points upwards, the undercarriage

The take-off

leaves the runway and 'bangs' might be heard as the suspension extends to its maximum.

V2 will shortly follow. This is the minimum speed at which the aircraft can safely climb away, at which point your flight has truly begun. All this in just a few seconds!

The climb

During the climb-out several events occur in rapid succession. The first is the retraction of the undercarriage (the wheels), which takes place as soon as the aircraft is established in a positive rate of climb, that is, heading upwards. You will hear and feel whirring, humming and clunking in the cabin as this happens. You might also notice trails of moisture (wing vortices) and misting above the wing. These effects are normal and occur when there is a lot of moisture in the air. At a safe height and speed the flaps and slats on the wings will be retracted according to a schedule for your particular aircraft. You will be aware of the vibration and noise this makes. The process of undercarriage, flap and slat retraction is called 'cleaning up', and the reduced drag allows the aircraft to climb more rapidly and to gain more speed.

At this time the pressurization of the cabin is begun. The cabin pressurization is managed by the environmental control system and operates continually. In older aircraft, the automatic cabin pressure control is directly related to aircraft altitude; in newer aircraft, such as the Boeing 777, the pressurization schedule can be set so that the cabin pressure increases smoothly to the setting planned for cruising altitude, even though the aircraft may achieve cruising altitude in a stepped climb. This steady increase of pressure minimizes discomfort among passengers from pressure changes, as does the distribution of sweets before take-off and descent to encourage swallowing at regular intervals. There is always more than one pressurization unit, should one fail, and they are powered by any engine.

You are likely to climb into clouds. Clouds always give rise to some turbulence and you can expect to be shaken around a little while you pass through them. Flight crew often look for a way to fly between clouds rather than through them to reduce the bumpiness. Anyway, you will soon be flying in the smoother air above them.

Once airborne, the flight crew might then significantly reduce the power to the engines to reduce environmental noise. You might be

aware of this somewhat alarming reduction in noise levels as well as a deceleration as the aircraft is flattened out a little into a more gradual climb. This is entirely normal and no cause for concern. The climb to cruising altitude is then likely to be uneventful. You might not even notice the aircraft levelling out. During the climb, when you are above any significant weather, you will be released from the mandatory requirement to wear your seat belt, but it is sensible to leave it loosely fastened while you are in your seat in case of any unexpected turbulence.

The cruise

The vast majority of your flight will be spent in the cruise at 30–40,000 feet. You are usually free to leave your seat while the going is smooth. However, despite flying above the weather, there may be pockets of clear air turbulence (CAT). CAT cannot be seen, nor can it be easily predicted or detected by current aircraft instruments, but laser forward-looking technology may solve this problem in the near future. CAT can make a smooth flight suddenly very bumpy. If preceding aircraft have already flown through it, they will warn following aircraft to try to avoid it. In any event, the captain or first officer will put the seat belt signs back on for you and will make sure they themselves are well strapped in. The flight attendants will also return to their seats and buckle up. Turbulence can throw the aircraft around and cause injury to anyone not secured in their seat but it cannot harm the aircraft, no matter how bumpy the ride. You are asked to return to your seat and put your seat belts on for your own safety, and for the safety of those around you.

During the long and often boring cruise, the flight crew can also relax a little, eat and visit the toilet. However, at all times, either the captain or the first officer is strapped into his or her seat and is monitoring the instruments and radio, even if the autopilot, now known as the flight management system, is keeping the aircraft straight, level and on course. This is a mandatory requirement set down in aviation law. The flight management system will also navigate and turn the aircraft at pre-selected positions (waypoints) during the flight.

Following the events of 11 September 2001, the flight deck is, unfortunately, no longer allowed to accept curious passengers, once an entertaining diversion for passengers and crew alike. The flight deck doors are now reinforced and bolted, and even the flight attendants must alert the flight crew if they wish to enter.

A note about the emergency exits and doors: contrary to popular belief, these cannot be opened in flight. The doors are of a plug-fit design and held in place by internal pressure. The pressure difference between the cabin and the upper troposphere or stratosphere makes opening the doors impossible.

The descent
As much as an hour or more before landing, the aircraft will begin its descent. The flight crew are requested by the air traffic control to descend, turn as necessary and hold altitude in stages. The flight crew usually do this via the control panel of the flight management system. The process of descending is considerably more drawn out than the climb and might be further lengthened by the need to circle in a stack of aircraft, all queuing in the air for their turn to land. The ride might become bumpy as the aircraft descends in stages through the cloud layer. The aircraft might even have to hold its altitude in cloud for a prolonged period while awaiting clearance to descend. You will have been requested to return to your seats and buckle up some time earlier.

During this phase the aircraft needs to be reconfigured for flying at the slower speeds needed for approach and landing. The operation of air brakes on top of the wings or at the back of the aircraft might be seen, heard and felt as the captain slows the aircraft. The flaps and slats will be lowered in stages accompanied by the whirring and humming with which you will now be familiar. The pressurization changes in the cabin will be felt in your ears as the pressure increases to the local ground level. The flight crew will complete the landing checklist at this stage.

The approach
The approach begins at approximately 10,000 feet above the ground, with about ten minutes to go to landing. At this time the cabin must be secured again. This means that your tray tables must be folded into the stowed position, your seat backs must be upright and your seat belts must be fastened. If the captain is not informed that the cabin is secure, for example even if a single tray table has not been folded away, he cannot land and will have no choice but to go around (see page 21).

At this stage the flaps are usually further deployed, and at about 1,500 to 2,000 feet above the ground the wheels will be lowered. This

The approach

often makes a very loud noise, and is accompanied by satisfying clunks as the undercarriage locks into place. The final approach ('finals') occurs in the last few miles after the aircraft has been prepared and all the checks are complete. You might again notice wing vortices and misting above the wing. The vortices generated by the flaps when coming in to land look like fuel leaking from the wing tanks, but rest assured that this is not what is happening. If the weather is clear the captain will be able to see the runway at this point, and will take over control of the aircraft from the flight management system and fly it manually, probably for the first time since soon after take-off. In most modern passenger jets and at bigger airports a system is also in place to land the aircraft automatically if necessary.

The landing

All pilots will, where weather permits, land the aircraft themselves. The flight management system will be disengaged during the approach and the aircraft flown onto the runway manually. In bad weather, such as when the cloud base is very low or fog prevents the runway being clearly seen, the flight crew might elect to let the automatic pilot land the aircraft. During every landing, however, the flight crew has to decide at a pre-selected 'decision height' whether or not to continue with the final approach. If the runway is not visible at this decision height or there is still a preceding aircraft on the runway, the flight crew will probably decide to abort the landing and go-around, or proceed to an alternative airport where the weather is better. In most cases, however, the runway and/or its lights will be visible and clear of aircraft and the landing will go ahead as planned. Decision height can be as low as 50 feet above the ground, even in the biggest commercial jets, and in some of the most modern aircraft there is no decision height. The flight crew can decide to go-around even after touchdown, an eventuality they train for repeatedly.

Soon after touchdown, the loud noise often heard from the engines is the flight crew engaging reverse thrust to slow the aircraft down rapidly. On longer runways in good weather, only very low thrust is applied in order to reduce noise, as the brakes are very efficient. You may also see the air brakes rise from the surface of the wing to help prevent the

The landing

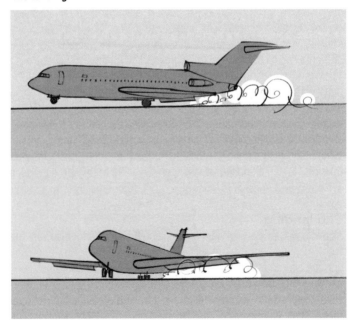

aircraft lifting off the runway again. The landing run is followed by another taxi to the stand, while outside the aircraft the slats and flaps hum and whir back to their cleaned-up positions. You are requested to remain seated with your seat belts fastened until the aircraft has reached the stand and the flight crew switch off the seat belt signs. This is for your own safety and the safety of anyone you would otherwise fall onto. Before the aircraft reaches the stand you will usually hear the command to 'set the doors to manual and cross check'. The flight attendants then disarm the doors so they can be opened safely.

The go-around

This is a rare and unexpected event and may give cause for concern. If there is any problem with the final approach, such as the previous aircraft has not cleared the runway or the flight crew decide to abort the landing because of bad weather, the captain will initiate the 'missed approach' procedure and go-around. This means to climb away, circle and make another approach to land on the same runway or at an alternative airport.

The passengers will notice a sudden change from a quiet approach to the noise of 'go-around power' (similar to take-off power) being applied to the engines. The landing gear will be simultaneously raised and the flaps and slats partially retracted. All the noises, clunks, hums and whirs come together and the aircraft points upwards and accelerates into the sky. The captain and first officer, who have trained for this eventuality time after time in the simulator, will be busier than at any other time in the flight and will not be able to give you any information at first. As they institute the 'missed approach' procedure, their priorities are to 'aviate, navigate and communicate', in that order. Passengers will be told what has happened and why only after air traffic control has been briefed. Pilots are very aware of the need to keep their passengers informed of what is going on, especially if it is out of the ordinary, but in this case it has to wait until a safe time. If you ever experience a go-around, you are unlikely to forget it in a hurry.

Now that you have a clearer understanding of the aircraft environment, both inside and outside, and the seven stages of flight, it is time to consider how to keep yourself as healthy as you can before, during and after your flight so that you arrive at your destination in good shape.

FLYING HEALTH – BEFORE YOU LEAVE

You can prepare yourself for your forthcoming flight during the weeks preceding your trip and during the time spent waiting at the airport. Depending on the nature of your trip, the length of your flight and your destination, your pre-travel preparation might include a visit to your doctor. This might be to arrange immunizations, anti-malarial tablets and repeat prescriptions of your usual medications for the period of travel, or to discuss any precautions that you, in particular, should take to reduce your risk of 'travellers' thrombosis' (deep vein thrombosis or DVT). You might shop for cases and carry-on luggage

Be prepared

Luggage with wheels

Comfortable, loose-fitting clothes

with wheels – avoid heavy, large, difficult-to-handle carry-on luggage since you will inevitably have to carry it at some point. You might also purchase neck pillows, hydrating face lotions and even herbal remedies designed to combat jet lag.

On the day of the flight, dress in loose-fitting, comfortable clothes made from natural fibres and make your way to the airport with plenty of time to spare. Try to avoid the stresses and strains of rushing if at all possible. Once at the airport, it is not too late to make your trip more comfortable. The airport lounges at most major airports around the world have shops and a pharmacy and you are certain to be able to purchase water for the flight. There should be time to relax, enjoy a light meal and ensure you are properly hydrated. You should avoid excessive alcohol consumption.

Planning your route

At this point it is worth considering the method and route of travel. If your trip is for pleasure and not too far, consider travelling by train, coach or even driving. A trip to Paris from

throw

Water

A VISIT TO YOUR DOCTOR

This might be necessary for any or all of the following reasons:

✈ You might require immunizations or anti-malarial prophylaxis (depending on your destination).

✈ You might wish to discuss the best ways for you to reduce the risk of DVT on a long-haul flight.

✈ You might want to know if it is safe for you to fly with a medical condition, and to get sufficient medication to cover the period of your absence and any emergencies.

✈ You might wish to discuss suitable sleeping preparations that would help you overcome jet lag.

London is as quick by train as by plane when the travelling time between the airport and the city centre is included.

Time spent in the thin air of the cruise and the number of depressurization and repressurization cycles as the aircraft climbs and descends are the most important factors in the development of ill health when flying. It is worth choosing as direct a flight as possible. A flight to a hub airport before the long-haul section of a flight, followed perhaps by a local onward connecting flight after the long-haul section, might be cheaper and/or unavoidable, but it means more time spent in the air and more take-offs and landings. A direct flight also reduces the chance of rushed transfers and even missed connections.

Travel to at-risk countries

Your doctor, specialist nurse or local travel clinic will be able to supply you with all your travel health needs. It is estimated that up to half of all travellers do not seek advice or preventative medical care prior to visiting health-risk countries. Even if you are travelling to a country generally considered safe, there may still be a few regions of high risk within that country, so be sure to detail your plans to the health-care professional. You might not know if a risk exists, which is why it is important to ask.

It is essential to plan ahead. Many immunizations must be administered at least six weeks before the date of travel to an at-risk area. Malaria tablets, where required, must be correctly taken: generally this means starting a week before travel to the at-risk area, taking them on a regular basis while there, and continuing to take them for a month after leaving. Do not forget that reducing the risk of malaria also involves taking precautions to avoid being bitten in the first place. A slight risk of malaria remains despite medical prophylaxis, but more to the point the bites itch unpleasantly, causing you to scratch and perhaps eventually to develop inflamed, swollen limbs and even infection. So consider insect repellents, mosquito nets and full-length cotton clothing at this stage.

DVT – 'travellers' thrombosis'

This topic is dealt with fully in pages 45–51, but if you are planning to travel on a long-haul flight, possibly to a country for which you need an immunization, and you are going to see your doctor or practice nurse, you should take the opportunity to ask about it. Your doctor

might recommend precautions for your particular needs. For example, if you have no allergy to aspirin, you might be recommended to take a small dose on the day before you fly in either direction, or even in the airport before you get on the aircraft. Your doctor might also recommend wearing special anti-DVT stockings on the flight.

DVT risk factors

It is most important to find out if you have a risk factor that makes you more susceptible to developing clots in the legs and then going on to develop travellers' thrombosis. If you are at high risk your doctor might recommend that you take special precautions to anti-coagulate ('thin') the blood to reduce the risk of clotting. The risk factors listed below are very general and the majority of those who fly probably fall into one category or another. Just because you have one or more of these risk factors does not mean you should not fly; it just means that you should be aware of the potential for DVT development and then take active steps to avoid it. The risk factors are:

- ✈ being a woman over 40 years of age
- ✈ having a personal or family history of DVT
- ✈ suffering from post-thrombotic syndrome or chronic venous insufficiency
- ✈ having a known abnormality of blood clotting that makes you more susceptible to a blood clot (such as antithrombin III, proteins or protein C deficiencies or factor V Leiden gene mutation)
- ✈ having had major surgery within the previous 2–3 weeks, especially to the abdomen or lower limbs, such as a hip replacement
- ✈ a current or previous malignancy (cancer)
- ✈ recent immobilization or bed rest for more than 24 hours
- ✈ being in a lower-limb plaster cast or having recently been in one
- ✈ being pregnant
- ✈ having varicose veins
- ✈ being a woman on the oral contraceptive pill or oestrogen-containing hormone replacement therapy
- ✈ some forms of heart and lung disease
- ✈ auto-immune disease, such as systemic lupus erythematosus (SLE)
- ✈ being overweight
- ✈ being a smoker

Medical conditions

The vast majority of people with medical conditions can fly as normal on passenger planes. However, the conditions inside the cabin at cruising altitudes, as outlined on pages 8–11, do necessitate special precautions in some circumstances. The cabin environment can exacerbate certain pre-existing medical conditions or trigger the onset of an acute problem in previously fit individuals. The airline wants you to have a safe, comfortable and uneventful journey. Help yourself by consulting your doctor or the airline's passenger medical unit if you have any doubt about your fitness to travel.

If you are recovering from a severe illness, a period of hospitalization or a major operation or injury, you should see your doctor for medical clearance before planning a flight; likewise, if a previously stable condition has deteriorated or become unstable, medical clearance should also be sought. Deterioration often occurs at the destination and complicates the return journey. This is an excellent reason for purchasing travel insurance that includes both health cover and repatriation, by air ambulance if necessary. Indeed everyone, regardless of state of health, should have adequate travel insurance – ensuring that any pre-existing conditions are declared.

Most patients with stable medical conditions can be accommodated by the major airlines. Any person who has special medical needs, such as oxygen or other medical equipment, or mobility problems, such as the need for a wheelchair or even a stretcher, should discuss these requirements with the airline. Passengers with most other disabilities can also be accommodated, but you will need an able-bodied escort to travel with you if you require assistance with your personal needs as the flight attendants will not be able to help you.

When not to fly

Patients with medical conditions will be assessed on an individual basis, as there are very few conditions that are likely to result in your never being able to fly. However, to avoid disappointment, here follows a list of acute conditions that are considered incompatible with flight in a passenger aircraft. Some can be accommodated with special precautions once medical clearance has been obtained, and others will resolve themselves or can be treated to enable flight at a later date. The conditions are:

- ✈ heart failure – uncontrolled
- ✈ heart attack – within 7 or more days of flight and only once back to normal activities
- ✈ stroke – until stable
- ✈ 'grand mal' epileptic fit – within 24 hours of flight
- ✈ respiratory disease – asthma, pneumonia, bronchitis and emphysema, causing shortness of breath at rest and/or after walking 50 yards on the flat or after climbing one flight of stairs
- ✈ pneumothorax – within 14 days of successful treatment to resolve it
- ✈ anaemia – a low haemoglobin concentration, below 7.5 g/dL (normal level is between 11.5 and 15.5 g/dL)
- ✈ sickle cell crisis – within 14 days of flight
- ✈ DVT – until the condition is stabilized on anti-coagulant (blood 'thinning') agents
- ✈ sinusitis and otitis media – until the condition is resolved
- ✈ tonsillectomy and middle ear surgery – within 10 days of the operation
- ✈ open eye surgery, for example, surgery for a detached retina – within 7–14 days of the operation or longer
- ✈ fractured jaw with wiring to hold the mouth closed
- ✈ fractured limbs – within 48 hours of the application of a plaster cast unless it is bi-valved
- ✈ full lower-leg plaster cast – some airlines may refuse to board any such passenger for safety reasons unless he/she travels on a stretcher
- ✈ major operations – within 7–14 days of flight, depending on the nature and extent of the operation
- ✈ infectious diseases
- ✈ singleton pregnancy – beyond the 36th week of gestation
- ✈ multiple pregnancy – consult your airline
- ✈ psychiatric disorders – psychoses or any unpredictable or aggressive behaviour problems
- ✈ drunkenness at boarding: you will be turned back

If in doubt, declare your condition to the airline when you book. Remember, an aircraft is designed to carry passengers safely, comfortably (within the constraints of cost-effectiveness) and uneventfully to your destination. It makes a poor ambulance, delivery suite or hospital.

Before you leave home

You do need to consider all flights as events in themselves, and not as an inconvenience between you and your business meetings or holiday nor as the start of your holiday fun. Flights can be very unpleasant events, especially if there are significant delays, in-flight diversions or landings at alternative airports. Most such eventualities are caused by the weather, but a passenger being taken ill on the flight is another possible problem. Even an uneventful long-haul flight can be tiring enough to make you change your plans at the destination in order to recover. So how can you minimize the impact of these inconveniences?

Medication: what to pack

Take only your own prescribed medicines in their original packaging and bring your prescription along so customs will not question what you have. Pack medicine in your carry-on bag, not your hold luggage, even if you think you won't need it during the journey. Even if you are sure you won't need it, imagine having to do without it in the event of prolonged delays without access to your luggage or even the loss of your luggage. Infrequently used asthma medication, for example, is often packed in the hold luggage, only for the otherwise fit, young and stable asthmatic to have an attack during the flight, often precipitated by the realization that the inhaler is in the hold and exacerbated by the stress of flying. Flight attendants have no access to the aircraft hold during a flight.

Diabetics and migraine sufferers are also strongly advised to have their medication with them even on the shortest flights. If you are recovering from a cold or have a blocked-up nose for another reason, you might benefit from nasal decongestants or inhalations of eucalyptus or mentholin. If you suffer from motion sickness, pack a preparation that can be taken before the flight or pressure-point wristbands if they help you.

Comfort on-board: what to pack

Airlines do their best to make your journey as comfortable as possible, though they must work within commercial constraints. Some passengers will, of course, be more comfortable than others, but this has cost them an awful lot of money. Short of upgrading your ticket, there are several steps you can take to improve the comfort of air

Medication – what to pack in your carry-on luggage

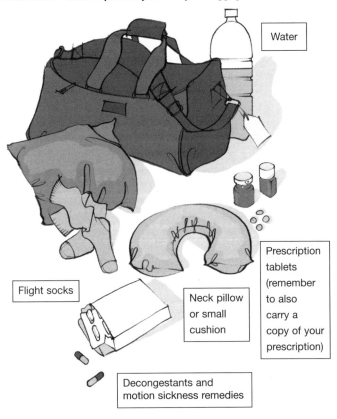

Water

Prescription
tablets
(remember
to also
carry a
copy of your
prescription)

Flight socks

Neck pillow
or small
cushion

Decongestants and
motion sickness remedies

travel. Consider including in your carry-on bag a neck pillow or small cushion to make your flight more comfortable. Flight socks or elastic support stockings to compress the leg and/or the Airogym (an inflatable exercise cushion) should also be considered to help reduce the chances of a clot forming, although there is no evidence to show that either is effective in reducing your chances of developing a DVT.

Wear layered, loose-fitting clothing with no tight belts or elastic. Wear natural fibres, especially close to the skin, so that you can stay comfortable, your skin can breathe and you can more easily regulate your temperature. Anticipate that once you are in the air doing little but sitting you will tend to cool down, so make sure you have sufficient layers to prevent getting cold. Ensure shoes are not too tightly fitting as your feet and ankles are likely to swell during the flight. If you like to remove your shoes during a flight and wear the socks supplied by many airlines, pack a pair of slippers in your carry-on bag so that you are free to move around the aircraft.

Consider packing lubricating eye drops, face and hand moisturizer and lip balm in your carry-on bag for comfort in the dry air of the cabin.

Getting to the airport and checking in

Leave in good time and anticipate the possibility of delays en route. Getting to the airport without hassle reduces stress levels, and if you make an early check-in you stand a better chance of getting the right seating for your needs. Unless you particularly like a window view and/or the proximity of a wall to lean on, the best all-round seat to choose is an aisle seat. This allows you not only to stretch your legs regularly while sitting down, but also to stand up and stretch or walk around at will. It is also an advantage when you need to make a call of nature. Occasionally you may be able to get one of the very limited number of seats in an emergency exit aisle or by a door that usually afford more leg room. These are allocated at the time of check-in to obviously fit, younger people, capable of opening the doors in an emergency.

Waiting to board

You should have a little time to kill before boarding, especially if you managed to check in early. Use this time to relax and perhaps have a light meal and a drink. You should aim to keep well hydrated throughout your journey as dehydration is difficult to avoid on prolonged flights and is a factor in many in-flight medical problems. It is best to avoid alcohol, which acts on the kidneys to produce more urine and therefore dehydrates you. Even beer will do this. In other words, you will eventually pee more volume than you drink. If you must have a tipple or two, compensate by drinking more water, both before and during the flight. Excessive alcohol consumption while waiting to board might result in your being prevented from boarding for safety reasons (and airlines are becoming increasingly likely to ban drunk passengers), as well as dehydrating you later.

You will probably be able do some last-minute shopping and preparation in the departure lounge to help you in-flight. You should buy some bottled (plastic) water to take on the flight. Although mineral water is usually available throughout the flight, obtaining regular refills can be difficult, so it is better to have your own supply. Drinking plenty of water during a long flight is probably one of the most important simple things you can do to remain fit and healthy. It will also ensure that you take a little regular exercise during the flight: to the toilet and back!

It is not too late to buy and take an aspirin if you have been recommended to do so by your doctor. Do not take an aspirin if you know you are allergic to it or suffer with stomach ulcers, are asthmatic or have kidney problems. Do not take an aspirin for the first time at this stage, as you do not want to find out after take-off that it has caused a problem.

Take advantage of your freedom and use the toilet at the gate before you board. There is often a considerable time between boarding, when the cabin attendants expect you to be seated and strapped in with your carry-on luggage stowed so that they can secure the cabin for departure, and the next opportunity to use the toilet on the aircraft.

Board in good time to find your seat and while there is still room in the overhead lockers for your carry-on bag. Avoid using the space under the seat in front of you for your bag because this only restricts your leg room. Take off your shoes, put on your flight socks and/or slippers, moisturize your face and lips, then make yourself as comfortable as possible. If you are desperate, the toilets may be used at this stage, but you will not make yourself popular with the flight attendants. Enjoy your flight!

When the doors are closed and the aircraft begins to move, you are now in a position to evaluate your situation. If you have empty seats around you, you might be able to spread yourself and your things around a little for extra comfort. This is likely to be the space you have to inhabit until you disembark, so make the most of it. Although as much as possible is done for the comfort of passengers, economic constraints apply, so the seat area you inhabit will often be cramped, you might not be able to stretch your legs out fully and you could be trapped between two strangers. For your own safety, you will often be required to wear your seat belt.

Then consider the cabin environment as a whole. The aisles are often blocked by the flight attendants while they go about their duties, the toilets may be few and occupied, and even if you have easy access to the aisle, it might not look much like a suitable area for a stroll. All this, and you have not even taken off yet. Do not despair, however. There are strategies you can adopt that will make your flight both more comfortable and safer for you, even in that austere environment.

Consider the flight as a separate part of your trip to be successfully negotiated on your way to better things, rather like passing an examination. Be proactive and then you can allow yourself to relax, safe in the knowledge that you are going to remain healthy while in the air.

Simple things can make a major difference to your comfort level. For example, if you strike up a conversation with the person or persons sitting next to you who block your access to the aisle it will be easier for you to disturb them later when you want to take a stroll or visit the toilet.

Hydration

The dry, thin cabin air means you lose more fluid over a prolonged period of flight than you might expect. Any substance with a diuretic effect – causing the kidneys to produce more urine – exacerbates this water loss. As we all know, diuretic substances are commonplace. The ones you will encounter on an aircraft include alcohol (a powerful diuretic) and the caffeine in coffee, tea and some

soft drinks. Caffeine is even present in chocolate and some frozen yoghurts. Alcohol and caffeine are the two most important causes of dehydration when flying.

So why does it matter if we become frazzled over the course of a flight? Well, excessive dehydration can cause the blood to thicken and this may lead to abnormally low blood flow in the veins, one of the three principal factors in the generation of thrombosis and DVT (see diagram on page 47). Dehydration also causes headaches and dry

HOW TO REMAIN WELL HYDRATED

✈ Bring your own supply of water aboard to drink during quiet times.

✈ Drink plenty of water or fruit juice.

✈ Avoid alcohol, especially in excess.

✈ Avoid foods and drinks that contain caffeine, such as tea, coffee, fizzy soft drinks and chocolate.

✈ Compensate for alcohol and caffeine by drinking extra water.

✈ Moisturize your face and lips regularly.

✈ Eat light meals and avoid salty foods, which will exacerbate the feeling of dryness.

✈ Eat fruit and vegetables if possible, because they have a high water content.

skin, particularly on exposed areas such as the face. Dehydration is one condition you can take active steps to avoid, and it only involves drinking water or fruit juice – hardly an imposition. Avoiding alcohol and caffeine, especially in excess, is vital but if you cannot resist a little tipple or your regular caffeine fix then compensate by drinking even more water.

Exercise

Prolonged sitting, especially in one position, is unnatural. Your body tells you this: you become uncomfortable and start wanting to move or get up and go for a walk. Even when you sleep, your body does not lie still for long. It's easy enough to get up and stretch or walk when you are at the office, but it is not so easy on an aircraft. The prolonged, enforced immobility of a long flight is exacerbated by cramped seating. Blood tends to pool in the deep veins of the legs when you are not active, and this pooling can theoretically be increased if you cross your legs and if the seat edge presses into the area behind the knee. The pooled blood in the legs is more sluggish and more prone to clot, potentially causing a deep vein thrombosis.

You can take active steps to avoid this. Most airlines today suggest simple exercises that can be done in your seat, and recommend that you stand up and/or walk around the aircraft cabin regularly. You will

Standing exercises

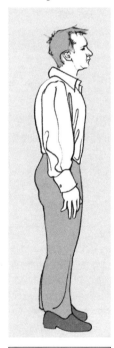 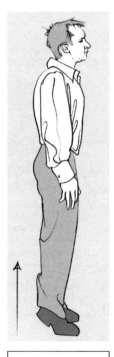 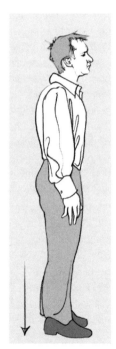

Stand with your feet flat on the floor and hip-width apart, keeping your back straight.

Keeping a straight back, raise yourself onto your toes.

Bring your feet back flat to the floor.

often find suggested exercises in the in-flight magazine; you might even have been sent details with your ticket. These exercises are designed to reduce the risk of a DVT. (For more information on DVT, see pages 45–51). Do the sitting exercises whenever you think of them, and at least once an hour. You may prefer to stand and walk around only when you visit the toilet, but if you are drinking plenty of fluids you will be doing this quite regularly anyway. Remember also to remove any clothes that cause a constriction around the legs, especially socks that are tight behind the knee.

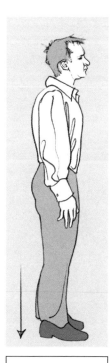

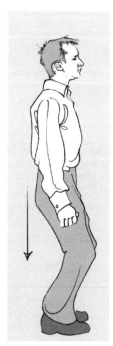

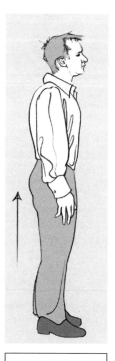

Stand with your feet flat on the floor and hip-width apart, keeping your back straight.

Bend your legs gently at the knees.

Slowly return to an upright position, keeping your back straight.

Feet and lower-leg exercises

Keeping your heels on the floor, raise both feet and toes as high as possible. Hold this stretch for 5 seconds.

Keeping the balls of your feet on the floor, raise both heels as high as possible. Hold this stretch for 5 seconds.

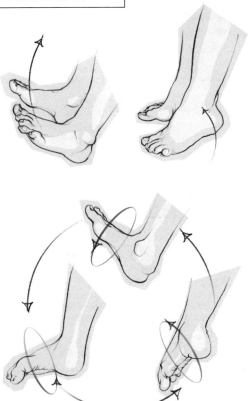

Lift your left foot off the floor and rotate your foot at the ankle clockwise 5 times and then anticlockwise 5 times. Repeat with your right foot.

Relax

It is also important to relax your body during the flight as your eyes, like your skin, will tend to become dry and even itchy. Relax with your eyes closed as much as possible and consider using lubricating eye drops. If you wear soft or disposable contact lenses the dryness might become more obvious because the lens will dry out more rapidly than your eye. Don't forget to take your contact lenses out if you wish to have a nap, unless they are designed to be left in when asleep.

Upper-body exercises

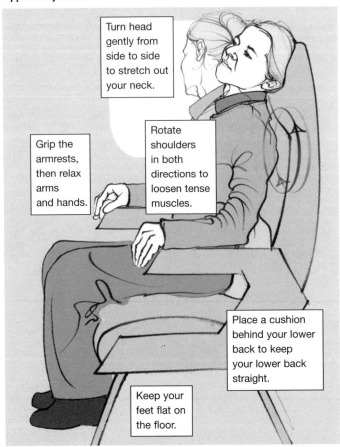

Turn head gently from side to side to stretch out your neck.

Grip the armrests, then relax arms and hands.

Rotate shoulders in both directions to loosen tense muscles.

Place a cushion behind your lower back to keep your lower back straight.

Keep your feet flat on the floor.

Get as comfortable as possible. Listen to music, watch a film or read a book. Try to have short naps if prolonged sleep is difficult. Remember, for safety reasons, you are not allowed to use the floor as a bed. If you do want to relax and sleep, keep your seat belt buckled and visible. Otherwise, if there is any turbulence, you will be woken and told to put your seat belt on. Eye masks and earplugs might be supplied in your personal pack and could be of use when you try to relax or sleep.

Medical care in the air

Perhaps one passenger in every 10–20,000 will become ill in the air, and approximately one flight in 7,500 will need to be diverted because

Medical kit

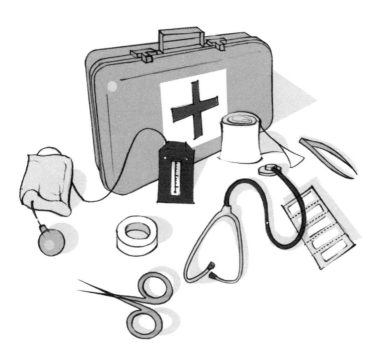

of such an emergency. The majority of illness, however, is minor in nature and includes fainting (the most common affliction, mainly a result of standing after prolonged immobility), diarrhoea and vomiting, headache, bruises and sprains. More major illness occasionally occurs, and typical problems include angina, heart attack, seizure and asthma. What can be done if you become ill on a flight? Probably more than you might imagine.

All flight attendants are required by aviation law to be trained in first aid and basic life support; the crews of some airlines provide intermediate life support. This training is refreshed annually.

The aircraft is also fitted with a medical kit, the minimum specification of which is laid down in aviation law. The medical kit on a long-haul flight contains the basic medical equipment a doctor or nurse might use for diagnostic purposes, such as a thermometer, a stethoscope and devices to measure blood pressure and glucose. It also contains dressings and drugs for many medical conditions, such as headache, motion sickness, blocked nasal, ear and sinus passages, asthma, allergy, diabetes, angina and other heart conditions. It might include equipment for minor surgery, intravenous infusion, splints for fractures and even basic things for delivering a baby.

Furthermore, most aircraft, especially on long-haul routes, carry an automated external defibrillator (AED) for use in the event of a sudden cardiac arrest. Flight attendants are trained in its use. There might also be the facility to monitor a heart rhythm or ECG and transmit it to doctors on the ground for diagnostic purposes. The crew are likely to have a link to ground-based medical support services that provide 24-hour telemedicine, linking the aircraft crew with physicians experienced in aviation medicine and able to provide remote advice.

Finally, a call can be put out to request any doctors on board to help in the event of an in-flight emergency that the aircrew cannot handle themselves. A doctor or other health professional who offers assistance is called a Good Samaritan. There are laws in many countries to protect a Good Samaritan who volunteers his medical expertise. It is estimated that there is a doctor on board on 60–85 per cent of flights, and it is reported that when a call for a doctor is made by cabin staff they obtain such voluntary help in 40 per cent of instances.

FLYING HEALTH – BACK ON THE GROUND

Once you have arrived at your destination, it is still important to consider your health. After all, you might not be in the best place to become ill. After a long-haul flight, you could be tired from lack of sleep, in a different time zone from your origin, standing outside in a climate for which you are not dressed. You are also probably somewhat dehydrated and stiff following your cramped journey. You would be ill advised at this point to climb into a rental car for a long drive to your final destination.

Recovery techniques

Getting back to normal

A few simple steps can help you return to normal as quickly as possible following your flight.

Once outside the aircraft you will be able to stretch your stiff limbs properly for the first time since boarding. Take advantage of this freedom to do the standing exercises illustrated on pages 34–5 to promote the flow of blood from your legs: walking, standing on your toes and stretching.

Take advantage of the airport facilities and get some more water to drink over the next few hours.

Be aware of the climate you are about to experience. Get appropriate clothing out of your reclaimed luggage and pack away unnecessary items before you leave the airport. The increase in perspiration in a hot country, especially if you are inappropriately dressed, will dehydrate you further, so make sure you are not too overdressed.

Avoid climbing into a car for another prolonged trip. Plan to stay locally overnight if you can, before embarking on a lengthy onward journey.

Sleep disturbance

After a long-haul flight most people experience jet lag, sleep disturbance or both. Getting over jet lag (circadian dysrhythmia) takes time. It is estimated that readjustment takes one day for each time zone crossed en route. Many frequent flyers take drugs such as melatonin or sleeping pills to accelerate their circadian adaptation – the process of getting over jet lag. Jet lag is dealt with in more detail on pages 56–9.

One of the major symptoms of jet lag is sleep disturbance. You might already have experienced one bad night's sleep on the aircraft so, whether or not you take active steps to combat jet lag, you are likely to experience some sleep disturbance following your trip.

Sleeping pills

Adults experiencing problems with sleep, especially when travelling, commonly use a variety of sleeping preparations. Over-the-counter medications commonly contain an antihistamine. This creates

IMPROVING YOUR SLEEP

Several measures can improve the quality of your sleep at your destination and they are relatively easy to do:

✈ Limit alcohol within two hours of bedtime because alcohol can result in a lighter, more disturbed sleep.

✈ Limit caffeine and tobacco within two hours of bedtime because these are stimulants.

✈ Avoid too much exercise close to bedtime. Although exercise will wear you out, it stimulates the body and mind and makes it harder to sleep.

✈ In a hotel, request a room away from noisy areas, such as lobbies and lift shafts, hang a 'do not disturb' sign on the door and request that reception hold your calls.

✈ Wear an eye mask if you expect to be sleeping when it is light outside.

✈ It is better to be slightly cool, with blankets available, than too warm.

✈ Maintain your usual bedtime routine, as far as you can.

✈ If you know sleeping is likely to be a problem for you, bring with you special comfort items, such as your own pillow or photos.

✈ If you cannot fall asleep, try relaxation techniques, such as those described on page 73, or you could even try listening to relaxation tapes.

✈ If you still cannot fall asleep, it is probably better to get up and do something gentle, such as reading, listening to music, watching television or solving a crossword, until you feel sleepy and ready to try again.

A good night's sleep

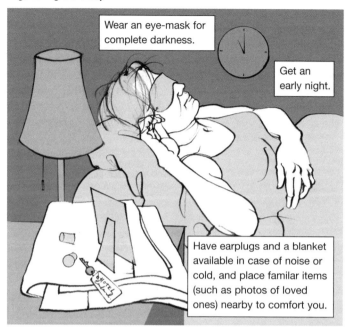

drowsiness and promotes sleep and has little effect on the nature of your sleep, nor any side effects. Prescription medications, however, might have a long active life in the body that causes a sedative effect into the following day – a sleeping pill 'hangover'. They might also change the nature of sleep, altering its quality such that you have problems the following day with attention and memory. Sleeping pills with minimal side effects are available. Check which preparation is best for you with your doctor, whom you should consult before starting any prescription or non-prescription medicine.

In general it is wise to test at home any medication, such as a sleeping pill, you plan to use on a trip. If it works at home, it will probably help on your trip and you will not be in for any surprises. Take the lowest effective dose for the shortest time possible and be aware of the possible side effects; these are printed on a leaflet with your medication. Avoid purchasing medicines abroad as they may not be the same preparation as you are used to or equally well regulated.

Caffeine

This is one of the most widely consumed substances in the world. Just as it can disturb your sleep at night, so it can help keep you alert during the day. Use caffeine strategically, especially after an overnight flight where your sleep was disrupted and you are suffering from jet lag. It takes about 15–30 minutes to work and lasts for about three to four hours, so plan when to take a dose to maximize its efficacy. It is found in coffee, tea, caffeinated cola drinks, chocolate and other foods, and in numerous over-the-counter preparations, such as stimulants, cold remedies and painkillers.

Alcohol

Alcohol is the world's number-one non-prescripition remedy for sleep-lessness. However, it must only be used sparingly in the hours before sleep as it will otherwise result in a lighter, more disrupted and less invigorating sleep.

FLYING CONCERNS

The major concerns regarding the possible effects of aircraft cabin environments on health, comfort and safety, as identified by the Medical Research Council in 2001, are these:

✈ travellers' thrombosis or deep vein thrombosis (DVT)
✈ cabin air quality
✈ the risk of infection
✈ cosmic radiation and magnetic fields
✈ jet lag

These concerns will be dealt with in more detail, one by one, starting with the most newsworthy in recent years: travellers' thrombosis.

Travellers' thrombosis

A physician who took a non-stop 14-hour flight in 1946 first identified this condition as a possible complication of air travel. In 1977 the term 'economy class syndrome' was coined, but it took until the turn of the 21st century for the problem of developing a potentially lethal deep vein thrombosis (DVT) during flight to come to the attention of the wider general public. The airlines have for some time accepted there was a link between immobility and DVT, and a link between long-haul flights and immobility. In a summit in 2002 attended by 16 major airlines, it was concluded that there was a possible link between DVT and air travel. The World Health Organization has also concluded that there is probably an association between long-haul travel and DVT, and is currently conducting studies that will hopefully conclusively confirm or discount this association.

Why does DVT occur in flight?

The term travellers' thrombosis (rather than 'economy class syndrome') is used here because it is the more accurate term, since DVT is by no means limited to the economy-class section of passenger aircraft. Indeed, travellers' thrombosis occurs in all classes of air travel and as a result of almost any form of prolonged immobility when travelling long distance by any means. The cabin environment on board a modern passenger aircraft, however, is unique, and the World Health Organization is currently carrying out research into whether it, in itself, increases the risk of developing a DVT. These particular aspects of the aircraft cabin environment have been suggested as contributory factors in the development of travellers' thrombosis:

 cramped seating

 prolonged immobility

 compression of the thighs and the back of the knee by the seat edge, and compression of the calf by the lower leg rest in business class

 the reduction in the level of oxygen compared to sea level

 the reduction in cabin pressure compared to sea level

 dehydration

These factors combined are unique to air travel. You will also notice that dehydration is the only factor that is under your direct and voluntary control.

What exactly is a DVT and how does it occur?

A thrombosis is an abnormal blood clot in the circulation. A venous thrombosis implies that the abnormal clot has formed in the venous part of the circulation (as opposed to an arterial thrombosis). A deep vein thrombosis occurs in the deep veins in the muscles (as opposed to within the superficial veins in the skin), most frequently in the muscles of the leg, especially at or above the level of the knee. Clots in the venous circulation form a cast of the inside of the vein (a thrombus), blocking it. The main danger with deep venous thromboses is that they can easily detach and travel within the circulation (embolize) until they impact in the lung: a pulmonary embolus. The severity of this condition relates to the size of the embolus (detached thrombus). Up to 80 per cent of pulmonary embolism is asymptomatic – you experience no symptoms and would have no idea it had occurred – but some can cause sudden death.

Three primary influences, known as Virchow's triad, assist in thrombus formation:

 injury to the inner lining of the vessel

 alterations of normal blood flow

 a state of enhanced blood clotting (hypercoagulability)

The first of these – injury to the lining of the vessel – is the most important factor in thrombus generation. It has been suggested that the rippling of the deep veins behind the knee in prolonged sitting may lead to damage in the vessel wall lining, though the significance of this

Virchow's triad in thrombosis

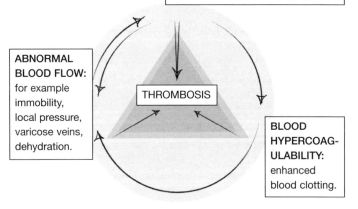

is unknown. The chemicals generated by smoking are also thought to injure the vessel wall lining. The second factor – alteration of the normal blood flow – might also result in injury to the inner vessel wall. Sluggish or turbulent blood flow, altered by immobility, prolonged seating and constricting clothes, for example, might cause a thrombus to form. The final influence is hypercoagulability: a state of enhanced blood clotting. It is thought that the reduced oxygen levels in flight might directly trigger such a state. Smoking again is thought to be harmful, as it is thought to promote coagulation (clotting) by an unknown mechanism.

There are also many medical conditions that are considered risk factors in the development of a DVT (see page 25).

Symptoms of a DVT

Half of all incidences of DVT are asymptomatic. The remainder may cause one or more of the following symptoms:

✈ swelling of the leg
✈ pain in the leg
✈ tenderness in the leg

- redness of the skin of the leg
- the leg is unusually warm to the touch
- pain in the calf on lifting up the toes or foot
- swollen veins in the skin (superficial veins)
- a raised temperature

Symptoms of a pulmonary embolus

Between 60 and 80 per cent of all pulmonary emboli are small and asymptomatic. The remainder might cause one or more of the following symptoms:

- a sudden cough
- coughing up blood
- chest pain or upper back pain
- shortness of breath
- a rapid heartbeat
- a raised temperature

Recent research into travellers' thrombosis

A recent study in the United Kingdom stated that up to 10 per cent of all long-haul airline passengers who did not wear elastic compression stockings had evidence of a symptomless DVT detected after their return trip. None of the patients reported in this study who developed a symptomless DVT had a pulmonary embolus, and indeed, were it not for the sensitive tests they underwent after their return, they would have been none the wiser. Nevertheless, the study suggested the potential for the development of symptomatic DVTs on long-haul flights. The authors of the study also admitted that this finding represented no risk to health and that spontaneous resolution would occur; in other words, that the DVT would disappear by itself without having caused any problems. None of the travellers who wore the class-I below-knee graduated elastic compression stockings developed a symptomless DVT: a significant finding, suggesting that wearing these stockings would be advisable for all long-haul flights. However, this study and others like it have been rightly criticized as insufficiently powerful to demonstrate a conclusive link between long-haul flights and DVT. This is why the outcome of the ongoing World Health Organization study into long-haul flights and DVT is considered so important.

Another recent study has shown that 72 per cent of the patients who developed a symptomatic DVT had at least one risk factor (hardly surprising, considering how many people have one or more – see page 25 for a list of risk factors). Even more significant was that 87 per cent of sufferers had undertaken long journeys made up of sequential flights, suggesting that there is an increased risk of DVT when you have two or more prolonged spells of relative immobility in close succession. Another study has highlighted a possible link between the cabin environment in particular – namely, the relative reduction in

---

PRE-FLIGHT ACTIONS TO AVOID TRAVELLERS' THROMBOSIS

✈ Consult your doctor or practice nurse if you believe that you have some of the risk factors for DVT (see page 25); he or she might advise you to take extra precautions.

✈ Take a low-dose aspirin before the flight if you can tolerate this drug and are not allergic to it. Aspirin is widely used to prevent abnormal clot formulation in the blood circulation, but there is no scientific proof that aspirin works in the prevention of DVT and the side effects of aspirin could be more harmful than a DVT.

✈ Buy and wear correctly fitted anti-embolism stockings. These can be prescribed by your doctor or purchased at your local pharmacy without prescription. Beware: poorly fitted stockings and those that ruck up behind the knee are probably more dangerous than no stockings.

✈ Buy the Airogym, an inflatable cushion for exercising your calves during flight (designed by a retired British Airways captain).

✈ Drink water and/or fruit juice, and buy some water to take on the flight.

✈ Avoid drinks containing alcohol or caffeine.

✈ Do not smoke.

oxygen levels – and a rise in the tendency of the blood to clot, one of the three primary influences in thrombus formation. They suggested that this, combined with being sedentary and dehydration, might cause an increase in travellers' thrombosis.

How to avoid travellers' thrombosis
There are numerous steps you can take to reduce your risk of travellers' thrombosis; most are simple measures that, with a little effort, may substantially reduce your chance of developing this condition, however there is no scientific proof of this. On pages 49–51 are lists of pre-flight, in-flight and post-flight actions.

Cabin air quality and transmission of infection
Cabin air at cruising altitudes around 39,000 feet is in some ways different from the fresh air we breathe at sea level. The lower pressure

---

IN-FLIGHT ACTIONS TO AVOID TRAVELLERS' THROMBOSIS

✈ Keep well hydrated with water and/or fruit juice throughout the flight.

✈ Avoid drinks containing alcohol or caffeine.

✈ Try to sit with good posture, with a cushion in the small of your back to maintain the natural curvature of the spine and your weight evenly distributed over your bottom. Try not to cross your legs, at least not for prolonged periods.

✈ Do regular leg and foot exercises in your seat, such as those illustrated on pages 34-6, or use your Airogym.

✈ Stand up at your seat and stretch your arms and legs, and get up and walk around the cabin as often as you can.

✈ Don't wear clothing that constricts the legs, especially at the back of the knee.

✈ Don't take sleeping pills, especially if you are in a cramped seat where movement is restricted.

and lower humidity are the most noticeable differences. Cabin air is also, however, very similar to the air on the ground. It contains the same proportions of the principal gases: oxygen (21 per cent), nitrogen (78 per cent) and others (1 per cent). As for the quality of the air, this is regulated by aviation law and controlled automatically by the cabin environmental control system. What is more, the captain, first officer and flight attendants all breathe the same cabin air as the passengers. There has, however, been considerable debate in the press about the recirculation of stale air in the cabin and the possibility that the environmental control system transmits infectious agents (such as the virus that causes severe acute respiratory syndrome or SARS) throughout the aircraft cabin.

Air circulation

Modern passenger jets automatically change the air inside the cabin every 2–3 minutes, providing plenty of air for each passenger (about 20 cubic feet per minute per passenger). Half of this is fresh air from outside the aircraft and half is recirculated through high efficiency particulate (HEPA) filters. These filters are the same as those routinely used in operating theatres to ensure that clean, infection-free air surrounds an open sterile wound during surgery. Provided they are regularly serviced and changed as required, HEPA filters remove 99.99 per cent of particles, especially bacteria. The filters may allow some small viruses through, but most viruses tend to clump together or stick to larger dust particles and thus get removed by the filters.

The recirculation of some cabin air is necessary mainly for economic reasons. An aircraft would use up a lot more fuel compressing and cooling sufficient air for the cabin if no recirculation were to occur. This does not make recirculation harmful to the passengers and crew, however. The total air exchange rate in an aircraft is over four times that in a building and twice that in an operating theatre. Recirculation also helps to conserve moisture and therefore maintains humidity at higher levels. Independent research has shown that the air in an aircraft cabin contains a considerably lower concentration of bugs compared to an inner city environment or the air on a bus or train. The World Health Organization has concluded that transmission of infectious diseases, including the virus that causes SARS, is not facilitated by the recirculation of air on aircraft.

Up to 70 per cent of complaints from passengers relate to infections such as colds and flu, or to headaches, nausea, vomiting, fatigue and dizziness, which they blame on the transmission of infection through the environmental control system or on poor cabin air quality. The cold or flu might have been contracted before boarding, however, and if picked up on the flight is more likely to result from normal airborne-droplet infection between people in close proximity for prolonged periods than from the spreading of germs by the aircraft environmental control system. Any such infection would have been spread in exactly the same way in an office, on a bus or at home. Other problems are attributable to the cabin environment – the lower pressure, the lower oxygen, the noise and vibration, the low humidity and the immobility – can all lead to fatigue, sleep disturbance and jet lag. Very little can be done about these factors, however.

Any person suffering from a contagious or communicable disease is requested by airlines not to fly because of the danger of infecting other passengers. Anyone with such a condition should inform the airline before they book a flight, and then obtain the necessary medical clearance once the condition has resolved before they fly. Permission to fly will usually be refused to families who have children with chickenpox and other communicable childhood diseases.

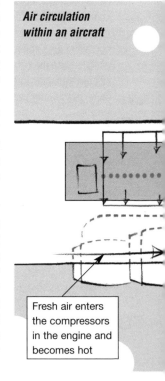

Air circulation within an aircraft

Fresh air enters the compressors in the engine and becomes hot

Keep yourself well hydrated and your face moisturized, and use a damp cloth or water spray to keep the membranes within your nose moist, and you may be better able to resist airborne-droplet infection from nearby fellow travellers with obvious colds.

Carbon dioxide

Carbon dioxide is a gas present in the air we breathe at a concentration of 0.03 per cent. It is produced as a product of normal metabolism by our bodies and excreted by our lungs. The air we breathe out contains about 4 per cent carbon dioxide. This gas is cleared from aircraft with the turnover of fresh air that occurs at 10 cubic feet per minute per person. This rate is twice that required to maintain carbon dioxide at safe levels as set down in aviation regulations.

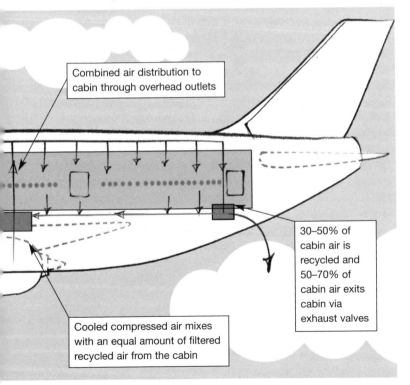

Combined air distribution to cabin through overhead outlets

30–50% of cabin air is recycled and 50–70% of cabin air exits cabin via exhaust valves

Cooled compressed air mixes with an equal amount of filtered recycled air from the cabin

Cosmic radiation

On Earth we are constantly exposed to ionizing radiation from various sources, especially some types of geological formation, such as granite. The overall background rate is approximately 2,600 microsieverts per year, but this varies from place to place. All ionizing radiation, including diagnostic X-rays, consists of particles that damage tissues as they pass through them. When you fly you are exposed to another sort of ionizing radiation: cosmic radiation. The rate of exposure to cosmic radiation is, on average for all flights, about 3–4 microsieverts per hour. By contrast, a diagnostic chest X-ray exposes you to between 100 and 200 microsieverts, equivalent to 25–60 hours of short-haul flying or 14–40 hours of long-haul flying, or, for argument's sake, a return transatlantic flight. An abdominal X-ray gives you a dose of about 1,000 microsieverts and a CT scan of the chest exposes you to between 2,000 and 4,000 microsieverts in one go, equivalent to 280–800 hours of long-haul flight.

Cosmic radiation comes from two sources. The larger source is outer space – galactic cosmic radiation – and the smaller source is the sun. The sun's lower-energy solar particles contribute relatively little to cosmic radiation except during solar flares. Cosmic rays are present in increasing quantities at increasing altitudes as the atmosphere and the Earth's magnetic field form protective layers. Unfortunately the aircraft body does not stop these cosmic rays.

Cosmic rays are measured in certain aircraft, and computer models can accurately estimate the dose received in the course of a flight. The computer programme takes into account all the factors that influence exposure to cosmic rays: the route flown, the flight profile, the time of year and the activity of the sun. On a long-haul flight the dose rate is estimated at 5–7 microsieverts per hour. The International Commission on Radiological Protection (ICRP) recommends an annual limit of 1,000 microsieverts for passengers, or 150–200 flying hours per year.

The maximum permitted exposure for aircrew is 20,000 microsieverts per year, but airlines impose their own maximum exposure of 6,000 microsieverts per year and ensure their aircrew are regularly monitored. Even regular ultra-long-haul aircrew are unlikely to exceed this airline maximum in a year.

Ionizing radiation damages cells as it passes through the body. It might result in the development of cancer, in genetic defects in

children conceived after either parent is exposed to ionizing radiation, and there is a risk to the health of the unborn child. It is estimated that the increased risk of developing a cancer as a result of exposure over 20 years of 5,000 microsieverts per year is 0.4 per cent. Thus the risk to aircrew, who may be exposed to this level of cosmic radiation over a career, is increased from 23 per cent (the average risk of developing a cancer) to 23.4 per cent. Likewise, the risk of a genetic defect in a child following the same career dose to a parent increases from 2 per cent to 2.1 per cent. The ICRP recommends a maximum exposure to the foetus during pregnancy of 1,000 microsieverts per year. Pregnant aircrew might, therefore, be transferred to ground duties.

Cosmic radiation is not constant, but filtered out by the atmosphere. When solar activity is at its greatest, galactic cosmic radiation is at a minimum. The Earth's magnetic field also protects us from cosmic radiation, and the magnetic fields are most effective over the equator. Therefore, the more northerly or southerly the latitude of your flight, the greater the rate of cosmic radiation.

The most recent period of maximum solar activity was in 2001, which unfortunately means that galactic cosmic radiation is on the increase again. Galactic cosmic radiation will reach a maximum in 2007, coinciding with a minimum in solar activity, and then decline again in this 11-year cycle to reach a minimum once more in 2012.

Solar flares and their associated proton events occur sporadically and without warning and can also significantly increase the dose of solar cosmic radiation up to rates of 100–1,000 microsieverts per hour or more at cruising altitudes for brief periods (minutes to hours). On Concorde, which uniquely flew at altitudes of up to 60,000 feet over northern latitudes, a dosimeter continuously monitored levels of cosmic radiation. At levels of 500 microsieverts per hour the captain would have had to obtain clearance to descend to safer, lower altitudes, but this never happened.

Since business travellers, unlike aircrew, have no annual limit of flying hours, they might unwittingly exceed the recommended annual exposure to cosmic radiation for passengers (1,000 microsieverts or 150–200 hours per year) and even the level recommended for aircrew (6,000 microsieverts per year or 950 flying hours per year). It is as well to be aware of this. Pregnant women need to be particularly careful that they do not fly excessive hours on business.

Magnetic fields

At home, or in the office, you are subject to the constant effect of the Earth's magnetic field. You cannot detect this but it can be measured: the norm is 1–3 milliGauss. On an aircraft, however, this value might increase, depending on your proximity to the flight deck. Because of the concentration of the aircraft's electrical system at the front, magnetic fields are significantly raised on the flight deck, in first class and in the front serving area. On some aircraft, magnetic field levels of 17 milliGauss are normal for the flight deck, 8 milliGauss for the front serving areas, 6 milliGauss in first class and 3 milliGauss or less in economy.

There is no proven association between exposure to magnetic fields and ill health, but the raised levels at the front of the passenger cabin of an aircraft are more than twice those at the back so, if you wish to avoid additional exposure, sit at the back.

The magnetic field of the Earth plays a much less significant role and affects all passengers and crew equally. However, flying around the equator will reduce the level of potentially harmful galactic cosmic radiation reaching your body, since it is here that the Earth's magnetic field is at its most efficient at preventing cosmic radiation from penetrating the atmosphere.

Jet lag

Most long-haul travellers will experience some sleep disturbance and many will also get jet lagged. In either case, you are unlikely to feel rested and alert when you arrive at your destination. More likely you will feel fatigued, apathetic and/or in a bad mood. You might suffer from stomach upsets and headaches. Decision-making, communication, memory and attention skills all suffer significantly – which is of particular relevance to the business traveller.

Your body's internal timekeeper (the supra-chiasmatic nucleus in the brain) is set by the pineal gland, which secretes melatonin when the day becomes dark. When you land at your destination, significantly east or west from your origin, your body is subjected to a new light–dark cycle, necessitating different sleeping and eating times. It takes a few days to readjust your circadian rhythm and synchronize your internal systems. While this adjustment occurs, you might experience difficulty in sleeping at night, staying awake during the day

and eating at mealtimes. In addition to the secretion of melatonin, your daily hormone, temperature and digestion cycles also need to readjust. This period of resynchronization, following a long flight across several time zones, is known as jet lag (circadian dysrhythmia).

Jet lag is often worse travelling east than west. This is because your body clock, uninfluenced by a light–dark cycle and the effects of the pineal gland, would still tick and would set a slightly longer day of 25–26 hours. Hence, for most people, a westerly flight, which lengthens your day, is less disruptive than an easterly flight. Furthermore, long-haul, easterly flights are often scheduled overnight, causing additional sleep disturbance. A north–south flight does not cause jet lag but will inevitably lead to some temporary sleep disruption, especially if the flight is overnight. These effects are shorter-lived and easier to overcome than jet lag.

Although it is not possible to abolish the effects of jet lag, there are various strategies that reduce its impact. Again, these strategies are divided into pre-flight, in-flight and post-flight periods.

SYMPTOMS OF JET LAG

✈ Sleep disturbance

✈ Daytime sleepiness

✈ Generalized malaise (a vague feeling of bodily discomfort)

✈ Reduced mental and physical performance

✈ Irritability

✈ Loss of appetite and gastro-intestinal complaints

Pre-flight strategies to reduce jet lag

✈ Choose a day flight, if available, rather than an overnighter. This will reduce sleep disruption and allow you to take some extra daytime rest during the flight.

✈ Be well rested prior to your flight by adopting good sleeping habits well before the departure date.

✈ Avoid caffeine in the hours prior to the flight if you intend to try to sleep. Caffeine is a stimulant that will reduce the quality of your sleep or hinder it altogether.

✈ Avoid smoking in the hours prior to the flight for the same reason.

✈ Avoid alcohol in the hours prior to the flight. Despite it being the world's number-one non-prescription remedy for sleeplessness, it results in lighter, more disrupted sleep.

In-flight strategies to reduce jet lag

✈ Try to nap or sleep by wearing an eye mask and using ear plugs, a neck pillow and a blanket.

✈ If sleep is not easy, try reading or listening to relaxing music, and keep yourself at a comfortable temperature.

✈ Keep well hydrated by drinking plenty of water.

✈ Avoid alcohol and caffeine.

✈ It is best to avoid the use of prescription sleeping pills as prolonged sleep in a confined space might be harmful and drowsiness is undesirable in the event of an emergency.

Post-flight strategies to reduce the effects of jet lag

✈ If you are going to be at your destination for only a short time before returning, consider maintaining your original time-zone sleeping and eating times.

✈ Take strategic naps of up to 45 minutes or short sleeps of up to 2 hours if you feel the effects of jet lag and sleep disruption.

✈ Use caffeine to help keep you awake and alert for meetings and driving. It takes about 15–30 minutes to work and lasts up to four hours.

✈ Take exercise, even a brisk walk in the fresh air, to help keep alert.

✈ Re-establish a good sleeping pattern as soon as possible to recover the sleep debt incurred as a result of the initial sleep disturbance of flying and the jet lag thereafter.

✈ Be aware that your body is naturally at its most sleepy between about 3am and 5am and again between about 3pm and 5pm. Likewise you are most alert between 8am and 10am and between 8pm and 10pm. So schedule business meetings during your 'alert' windows and naps during your 'sleepy' times.

✈ Keep well hydrated.

✈ Use over-the-counter sleep medications, which usually contain antihistamine to promote drowsiness and sleep, if necessary.

✈ Use prescription sleeping pills only on the advice of your doctor and avoid the concomitant use of alcohol.

Melatonin

Melatonin is a natural hormone produced by the pineal gland in the brain. It has a central role in setting the circadian rhythm of our bodies to the dark–light cycle of the 24-hour day and other external so-called 'zeitgebers'. Melatonin tablets can be purchased at health food shops in some countries, such as the United Kingdom and the United States, but not in others. Some frequent long-haul travellers use melatonin tablets to achieve a faster body-clock realignment.

Melatonin tablets are used in two main ways: to promote sleep and to combat jet lag. Research suggests that melatonin might reduce the effects of jet lag by promoting sleep when it is taken close to the target bedtime at the destination, between 10pm and midnight, and that it is more effective in decreasing jet lag after flights crossing five or more time zones, particularly when flying in an easterly direction. A dose of anywhere between 0.5 and 5mg was found to be adequate; the higher the dose the faster sleep was induced and the better the quality of sleep. Doses greater than 5mg did not make any further difference.

Other research has shown that the timed use of melatonin can hasten the resynchronization of the circadian rhythms. This involves taking the tablet in the early evening on the day before an eastbound flight, and again before bedtime at the destination for a few days until you are over the jet lag. This way the dose of melatonin brings the body clock forward, rather than relying on the body's own melatonin production to catch up. Flying west, however, is a little more complex, as it is necessary to take the melatonin in the early morning on the day of your departure and then at mid-morning or later at your destination, prolonging the 'night' in the eyes of your body clock and lengthening the day. You can take it earlier each morning and then stop when you are readjusted. The major disadvantage of this is that melatonin aids sleep, and the main side effect is reduced alertness and performance during the morning. It is not permitted for aircrew for this reason.

Melatonin can have adverse effects if you are epileptic and it can interfere with warfarin (a blood 'thinning' drug) and the reproductive system. In any case, you should discuss using any new over-the-counter medication with your doctor or pharmacist before you travel.

FLYING ISSUES

In addition to the five major health concerns outlined in the last chapter, there are several other issues that surround flying and relate to your health in the air:

➤ aircraft disinsection
➤ airsickness
➤ swollen ankles or 'jet flight leg'
➤ seat pitch
➤ ozone
➤ emergency oxygen
➤ in-flight safety

Aircraft disinsection

This term refers to the spraying of the aircraft cabin prior to landing to kill any mosquitoes or other insects that have stowed away on the aircraft. It is necessary when travelling from a country with a mosquito-borne disease problem, such as malaria or dengue fever, to another country usually without such a problem, although some countries insist that all aircraft are sprayed regardless of origin. You might not have thought the country you departed from had such a problem, especially if you were not advised to take anti-malarial prophylaxis while there. If disinsection occurs prior to landing at your destination, it means that there may be pockets of malaria or dengue fever in parts of the country you left. This is to protect the destination country against possible epidemics.

The World Health Organization requires airlines to spray on certain routes to comply with international health regulations, but the final decision to spray a particular flight is made by the authority responsible for the airport. Failure to disinsect a flight might result in disembarkation being refused until the local Port Health officials have completed their own disinsection process.

The aerosol sprays used contain an insecticide, a solvent and a propellant. These days the solvent and propellant are non-ozone depleting. The World Health Organization designates the contents of the sprays and has determined that there is no evidence to suggest that the insecticide they specify presents any toxic hazard to the passengers or crew when used correctly. Furthermore, before disinsection spraying occurs, an announcement must be made to allow passengers to cover their noses and mouths and shut their eyes, if they so wish, for the few minutes the spray takes to dissipate.

To avoid inhaling the droplets containing insecticide you need only take the same measures as you might to avoid breathing in after someone else has sneezed, namely to cover your nose and mouth with a moist handkerchief or tissue that will filter out the droplets. You will avoid any irritation of your eyes if you shut them temporarily, especially if you wear contact lenses.

Airsickness

This is no longer a major problem for airlines. Advances in aviation technology and design, principally the ability to fly at greater altitudes and thereby avoid most of the turbulent air, have reduced the incidence of airsickness among passengers and crew. Furthermore, passengers have an increased opportunity to fly and become accustomed to flying conditions. Most commercial passenger airsickness now occurs on short-haul flights on turbo-prop aircraft that fly at altitudes of between 8,000 and 25,000 feet.

Airsickness is principally caused by low-frequency motions of the aircraft, predominantly in the vertical and lateral planes, and is especially noticeable in the climb and descent through the more turbulent air at lower altitudes, although it can also be induced by the clear air turbulence at higher, cruising altitudes.

There is contradictory evidence over the effect of your seating position on airsickness. In general it is

---

AIRSICKNESS SYMPTOMS

If you are unlucky enough to suffer from motion sickness, or if you take a flight with particularly bad turbulence, you might experience one or more of the symptoms below:

- ✈ *Nausea*
- ✈ *Vomiting*
- ✈ *Dizziness*
- ✈ *Drowsiness*
- ✈ *Increased salivation*
- ✈ *Headaches*
- ✈ *Feeling hot and/or sweating*

thought that sitting at the front or over the wing can reduce the incidence of airsickness. Moderate levels of alcohol consumption are thought to have little or no effect on airsickness.

To reduce your chance of becoming ill, consider the following measures:

✈ avoid short-haul flights in turboprop aircraft
✈ eat lightly before your flight
✈ keep active during your flight, by reading, for example
✈ use anti-motion sickness medication as recommended by your doctor or pharmacist, bearing in mind that its use can cause drowsiness and you might have to drive at your destination

Swollen ankles

Sitting for prolonged periods with your legs dangling down can cause ankles and lower legs to swell. This condition is known as 'jet flight leg'. Fluid that is naturally squeezed out of the blood vessels is not pumped back up the leg and back into the circulation while your legs are below your heart level and inactive. The anti-gravity pump is

normally provided by the contraction of muscles when you walk. Swelling will be dependent on how much of the time you spend seated, how much you get up to walk around and, to a lesser extent, whether you perform any of the exercises described on pages 34–6. Swelling

will also tend to be worse on overnight flights because you want to sleep and are reluctant to disturb others sleeping around you, so you tend to remain seated for longer. These factors are under your control.

Ankle swelling is usually only noticed after three hours of flight and will become worse as the flight goes on. It is more common in women over 30 and in people with varicose veins. As the condition is exacerbated by the reduction in pressure in the cabin at cruising altitudes, it tends to be worse on long-haul flights, which cruise at the highest altitudes. A hot cabin temperature will not help either. These factors are not under your control.

Seat pitch

Seat pitch is the distance between any point on one seat and the same point on the seat in front. Seat pitch is regulated for reasons of safety, not comfort, and relates to the robustness of passenger seats and the ease of evacuation in an emergency. In economy class on a scheduled airline the seat pitch will be between 30 and 34 inches. Close seat pitch is associated with poor seat comfort and necessarily restricts the degree of recline that is much appreciated for night travel; it also prevents the correct adoption of the brace position in all but the shortest people.

With long-haul flights getting ever longer, space is of considerable concern to the passenger – and the airlines – because of the risk of travellers' thrombosis. There is no evidence, however, of any link between seat pitch and DVT. In surveys, leg room and seat comfort are consistently rated as the two worst aspects of air travel.

Your seat

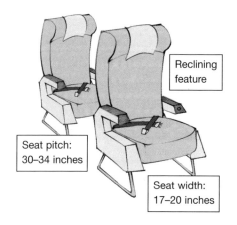

Reclining feature

Seat pitch: 30–34 inches

Seat width: 17–20 inches

Seat width is another important factor. The minimum recommendation is 17 inches but economy seats can vary between 15½ and 20 inches. Cramped seating increases discomfort and can make it difficult to leave the seat to take recommended exercise.

Ozone

Ozone is a toxic air pollutant that causes inflammation of the respiratory tract at low concentrations. It is generated by the action of ultraviolet radiation on the molecules of oxygen present in the upper atmosphere. Fortunately, the ultraviolet radiation is filtered out as it passes through the atmosphere and so does not generate ozone in the lower atmosphere. Ozone is at its greatest at the poles and has a seasonal maximum in the spring. Aircraft fly through the upper atmosphere, often over the poles, through an atmosphere higher in ozone. Fortunately, the ozone is broken down into oxygen molecules by the heating of the air in the engine compressors prior to cooling, conditioning and entering the incoming cabin air stream.

Emergency oxygen

All aircraft carry an emergency supply of oxygen that automatically drops down from the panel overhead in the unlikely event of a sudden cabin depressurization. If the cabin fills with smoke the oxygen masks will be deployed manually. This oxygen supply is essential, as if the pressure in the cabin suddenly drops at altitude there will soon be insufficient oxygen in the cabin environment. Without additional oxygen you would become unconscious within a minute at normal cruising altitudes. Put your mask on immediately in order to be able to help others. (See page 79.)

In the meantime, the flight crew will put the aircraft into an emergency descent in order to reach an altitude at which it is safe to breathe without additional oxygen: 15,000 feet above sea level or less. The captain and first officer will also be wearing their oxygen masks and breathing the same 100 per cent oxygen as you. Since the aircraft is under their control, the oxygen delivery system available to the flight deck is separate from, and a little more complex than, yours, being able to deliver 100 per cent oxygen at positive pressure if necessary. It is imperative that the captain and first officer remain conscious and at peak performance throughout.

Some safety issues

There is increasing concern within the airline industry that people are bringing more and more hand luggage onto the aircraft. Safe stowage space is at a premium, and, even then, in severe turbulence it is possible for overloaded overhead lockers to open and disgorge their contents. The main danger with overloaded overhead lockers is that when they are opened in flight or upon disembarkation, their contents, disturbed by turbulence, come tumbling out. Some items, particularly bottles of duty-free goods, can cause serious injury. Furthermore, baggage stowed on the floor tends to block emergency exits and hinder evacuation in the event of an emergency. It is possible that airlines might reduce carry-on allowance in the future, and perhaps make a provision that duty-free items be stowed in the hold with the luggage.

Unexpected turbulence can lead to serious and even fatal consequences for passengers who are not seated. Those seated are at less risk of injury, but a fastened seat belt offers additional protection. Airlines advise you to keep your seat belt fastened at all times for your safety, although this represents something of an infringement of your (already limited) freedom on an aircraft. In the future, however, it might become a mandatory requirement for all passengers while seated.

Airlines are also increasingly concerned with the incidence of drunk and/or unruly passengers and air rage. These passengers represent a safety hazard to the aircraft, as has been demonstrated on a few occasions in recent years, and such people are more likely to be forcibly restrained in the future and the aircraft diverted, if necessary, to disembark them. The Federal Aviation Authority reported between 150 and 300 enforcement actions to control unruly passengers per

Stowing hand luggage

Overhead lockers must be packed carefully to avoid heavy items coming loose during turbulent flights.

Luggage must not be allowed to block emergency exits.

year between 1995 and 2001. Assaulting, threatening, intimidating or interfering with a crew member in the performance of his or her duties aboard an aircraft being operated is a federal offence. Passengers engaging in such unruly behaviour can face a fine of up to US $25,000 per offence or a criminal prosecution. One incident can result in multiple violations. Furthermore, if an aircraft is diverted, the airline may pursue legal action to recover the very substantial costs incurred.

FLYING FEAR

Fear of flying is very common. It is estimated that up to 40 per cent of people are uncomfortable with flying and up to one in every six adults in America avoids flying because of fear: that is, 25 million Americans. Fear of flying is, in fact, a specific phobia, a type of anxiety disorder. Anxiety is the fear of what might happen rather than what is actually happening. In other words, an anxious passenger is abnormally afraid of what could happen on an aircraft that is functioning perfectly normally. On the other hand, feeling fear when there is a clear and present danger, such as when a pilot is making an emergency landing, is normal.

In general, people become uncomfortable about flying; it is not an inborn characteristic. Fear of flying usually starts at about 27 years of age. It tends to be associated with the accumulation of weighty responsibilities through life, such as a spouse and children, and a heightened awareness of the fragility of life as one gets older. These fears can eventually translate into a fear of flying.

The fear

Fear of flying consists of several components, not all of which are specific to flight. Thus it might include anxieties about any of the following: lack of control; heights; being trapped; enclosed spaces; crowds; nausea; panic attacks and embarrassment; take-offs and landings; weather and turbulence; flying over water; lack of understanding of the reasons for the actions, sounds and sensations going on around you; being dependent on the good judgement of the airline industry, the aircraft engineers, the pilot and the air traffic controllers and on the integrity of the aircraft; fear of abandoning your loved ones, possibly for ever; terrorism, especially following the events of 11 September 2001; crashing; and dying.

This chapter discusses some of the causes of aviophobia (fear of flying), some of the typical symptoms and, finally, strategies you can use to overcome any discomfort, or fear, you have about flying.

The causes of fear of flying

You might be able to pinpoint exactly when and why you became afraid of flying, but this is quite rare. More commonly you will be able to identify one or more of the following circumstances that first contributed to your problem: you previously experienced a difficult flight; you heard stories of difficult flights; you developed other problems that increased your fears of flying; and/or you experienced a stressful time in your life in the months before becoming afraid of flying.

Serious problems are very rare on passenger flights. Most people who have a fear of flying have never experienced real danger in flight. A frightening experience on a flight is more common – however, it is you who decides what is frightening in your mind and many such experiences present no actual danger to your life or health. Nevertheless, you will feel scared and remember the experience as a difficult and dangerous flight. As a result you might worry about future flights and become fearful if the same set of circumstances (such as turbulence) occurs, or seems likely to occur, for example if the captain warns you to return to your seat and fasten your seat belt.

Any fatal aircraft accident gets disproportionately heavy press coverage. Cancer and heart disease, for example, which are the biggest killers in the western world, get much less coverage. It is therefore quite common to hear about other people's problems during flight. If you imagine yourself having the same experiences, your body will react and you will feel anxious. You might translate this anxiety into worry about your next flight. You might seek information to reinforce your anxieties and ignore safety information, thus bolstering your fears and further contributing to the discomfort you feel when flying.

If you already have a fear of loss of control, such as being trapped in enclosed spaces or heights, then the aircraft cabin is unlikely to be a place you will enjoy being in, especially as it is usually full of strangers. If you have suffered from panic attacks in the past, for example, before public speaking engagements, the fear that you might embarrass yourself by having an attack in the aircraft will contribute to your fear of flying. Most people who suffer from panic attacks derive comfort from their ability to escape the fearful place easily. An aircraft cabin is not such a place. The more you worry about panic attacks, the greater the likelihood of one occurring. To stop flying altogether would be the only remaining way to

FEAR OF FLYING SYMPTOMS

Anxiety causes two types of symptoms, physiological and psychological.

Physiological symptoms might include:

✈ *Sweating*

✈ *Dry mouth*

✈ *Prickly sensations over the trunk*

✈ *Dizziness*

✈ *Weakness*

✈ *Muscle tension and tremors*

✈ *Laboured breathing and overbreathing*

✈ *Tingling and numbness around the mouth and fingers*

✈ *Spasm in the muscles of the hands and feet*

✈ *Heart palpitations and chest pain*

✈ *Abdominal discomfort*

Psychological symptoms might include:

✈ *Impaired memory*

✈ *Narrowed perceptions*

✈ *Poor or clouded judgement*

✈ *Repetitive, negative thoughts*

prevent the build-up of overwhelming anxiety.

Prolonged periods of stress in your life can lead to a fear of flying. Stressors include major life events, such as bereavement, marriage, divorce, moving house, changing jobs and even having children. All are associated with some form of loss, even if it is just a loss of a degree of freedom. During these stressful times you may become more fragile and you may also begin to fear the feeling of being trapped or out of control. These are typical fears associated with flying, and so it is easy to develop a fear of flying at these times when your self-confidence is at a low ebb.

Many people fear flying because they naturally fear the unknown. A lack of understanding or even misinformation about how aircraft fly does not help the potential passenger who looks at an enormous aircraft on the ground and tries to imagine how it gets up into the air and stays there (see page 75 to find out how it does).

Once someone has developed a fear of flying, logic does not get much of a look-in. Flying is 20–30 times safer than driving a car, but the sufferer will drive a car daily without fear and yet avoid flying. Or

Diversionary tactics

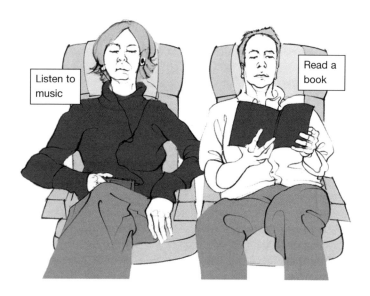

Listen to music

Read a book

Eat a snack, do some work or play games

worse, the sufferer continues to fly, but struggles against this sense of fear and thus reinforces it.

Strategies to overcome fear of flying

Fear of flying can be very difficult to overcome for several reasons. Your fear of flying might be multifactorial, involving some or many of the components given at the beginning of this chapter. Media coverage of aircraft accidents is out of proportion to the number of fatalities compared to other killers, such as car accidents, and this can reinforce your perception that flying is risky. Your perception of risk is paradoxically – the opposite of logically – high because you are not in control (unlike when you drive a car) and you may have little conception of how aircraft work; the level of risk is an unknown quantity but what you do know is that any adverse outcome would be severe. It is also difficult to confront your fears gradually because flying is an all-or-nothing event. Becoming accustomed to flying can be an expensive undertaking.

It is beyond the scope of this book to consider in detail the psychology of this anxiety disorder and how to overcome it; there are numerous other books and websites on this subject that might be consulted. In addition, most major airlines run courses specifically tailored to the needs of those who have a fear of flying. These courses usually last one day and consist of extensive preparation by a clinical psychologist and highly experienced pilots, followed by a short flight.

Ways to reduce anxiety while in the aircraft

There are ways in which you can reduce your feelings of anxiety while in the aircraft. Notice and accept your feelings of anxiety or panic. Do not fight them, because that will make them worse. Instead, say to yourself: 'It's OK to be nervous but I can handle this.' Acceptance helps stop the feelings of discomfort from spiralling out of control and giving your body the signal that this is an emergency, which would give rise to the symptoms of anxiety listed on page 69.

Diversionary tactics

Chat to your neighbour

Once you have noticed and accepted your feelings of discomfort, you will be in a better position to calm yourself down and avoid the symptoms of the emergency response. Think about your breathing rate and depth. Avoid rapid, shallow breaths and concentrate instead on breathing normally, or take a long breath in through your nose, hold it for a count of three and then exhale through the mouth slowly while you relax the muscles in your face, shoulders and abdomen. Repeat this several times and then breathe normally. Concentrate on your breathing for a while and try to avoid distressing thoughts.

Try some relaxation techniques. To help you feel more relaxed it is first necessary to feel the tension in your muscles. Select a group of muscles: for example, squeeze your eyes shut or grip the arm rests with your hands. Hold the squeeze for a slow count to ten while concentrating on your breathing, then relax your muscles and exhale slowly. Repeat this two more times before finishing off by circling your head, shoulders and ankles (see diagram on page 37). Then close your eyes and feel the weight of your relaxed body.

Breathing technique

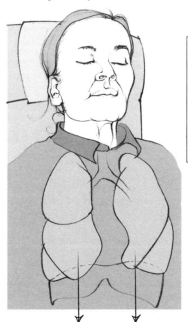

Breathe slowly and deeply. Take a long shallow breath through the nose, hold for a count of three and then exhale slowly through the mouth while relaxing muscles in the face, shoulders and abdomen. Repeat until calm.

Other measures that may help include diversionary tactics, such as reading a book, doing a crossword or getting on with work you brought with you. Talk to your neighbour, observe other relaxed passengers and raise any specific concerns with a flight attendant. Have a snack and drink some water or fruit juice. Perform the exercises designed to avoid DVT (see pages 34–7) and stand up, stretch your legs or go for a walk. Finally, avoid alcohol and caffeine.

The anxiety of flying can be reduced or eliminated by getting involved in activities, rather than sitting there quietly worrying. Trust the airline industry, accept your fears and manage them, breathe, relax and divert yourself.

AIRLINE INDUSTRY FACTS

Once you have become motivated to fly and determined to overcome your fears, the first and probably the most crucial step is to develop trust in the airline industry. The following facts might help:

✈ Flying is the safest mode of modern transport, 20 to 30 times safer than driving a car.

✈ It costs a similar amount to train a pilot as it does to train a doctor.

✈ Modern passenger aircraft have at least one back-up for virtually every essential system. For example, there are three flight management system (autopilot) computers.

✈ Passenger aircraft undergo, on average, 12 hours of maintenance for every flying hour.

✈ Aircraft are manufactured to withstand more than five times (and up to 15 times) the strongest measured level of turbulence.

✈ Most airlines and most aircraft types have a fatal-event rate of fewer than one in every million flights.

FLYING QUESTIONS

It is hoped that most of your questions about flying and, in particular, about healthy flying have already been answered in the previous chapters. However, during the research for this book, a number of questions relating to flying emerged, for which this chapter provides some basic answers.

🅀 HOW DO AIRCRAFT FLY?

The wings of an aircraft generate lift thanks to their special aerofoil shape: curved on the top and flat underneath. Air passing over the wing has to travel further than the air passing beneath it, so it has to speed up. This causes the pressure above the wing to be less than the pressure beneath, which effectively sucks the wing upwards.

The engines generate thrust that pushes the wings through the air, creating the flow of air over the wings that generates lift. When the lift is greater than the weight of the aircraft, it will fly. The engines continue to power the aircraft as the drag created by the movement of the aircraft through the air must be overcome to prevent a stall. Stalling is when the flow of air over the wings becomes turbulent due to the aircraft travelling too slowly or at too steep an angle of climb for the wings to generate lift. Computers prevent this from occurring, even accidentally, but recovery from a stall is easily done: by pointing the nose down and applying more power.

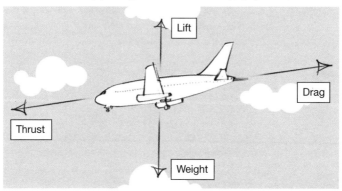

Q HOW DO THE ENGINES WORK?

Jet engines are quite simple and very reliable. They are huge, powered fans. One of Newton's three laws of motion states that 'to every action there is an equal and opposite reaction'. This means that if you apply a force in one direction, you will be forced back in the opposite direction by an equal amount. So, if you push something out of the back of an engine, it will create an equal amount of forward force. A jet engine pushes mainly air out of the back, air that is sucked in by the huge fan at the front of the engine. The air is compressed and accelerated in the engine by the turbine that also drives the fan. The turbine is itself powered by burning fuel in the compressed air. The force of the air pushed out of the back of the engine is proportional to the mass of the air and its speed (squared). Hence jet engines are often called turbofans.

Q CAN AIRCRAFT RUN OUT OF FUEL?

Complex calculations are performed before the aircraft takes off to work out the quantity of fuel required for the flight based on the weight of the aircraft, weather conditions, especially headwinds, and the distance to be travelled. Then an additional amount of fuel is added to allow for a landing at an alternative airport, if required. This is expensive because it means transporting extra weight but it is enforced in aviation law. Finally, if the fuel situation becomes critical for any unforeseen reason, the captain will declare an emergency and will be given priority to land. It is possible for an aircraft to run out of fuel, but it is exceedingly rare.

Q CAN AIRCRAFT RUN OUT OF BREATH-ABLE AIR?

No, is the short answer. Aircraft take air from outside, through the engines, compress it, cool it and conduct it into the cabin; therefore the air supply is unlimited. In the unlikely event of a sudden cabin depressurization or the cabin filling with smoke, oxygen masks will drop down from the panel above your head. This supply is limited, as it is stored in oxygen cylinders, but it is sufficient for the duration of an emergency.

Q WHERE IS THE SAFEST PLACE TO SIT ON AN AIRCRAFT?

There is no safest seat. The nature and extent of injury and fatalities in any aircraft emergency depend on the cause of the disaster and the effect of the damage to the aircraft. Numerous factors influence the survival of the passengers in an accident regardless of seating position. For example, in any major accident, fire and heavy smoke are likely to be significant dangers. Survival in this situation will depend on the ability of the crew and passengers to stay calm and to leave the aircraft quickly via the nearest available emergency exit. Another significant source of injury is heavy items of hand luggage in the overhead lockers, such as bottles of duty-free spirits, which can become missiles within the cabin during an accident.

Q DO MOST PEOPLE DIE IN AN AIRCRAFT CRASH?

Between 1978 and 1995, there were 164 accidents around the world involving jet aircraft designed and built in Western Europe or the US that resulted in the fatality of at least one passenger. The percentage of passenger fatalities was:

✈ in 41 per cent of accidents all passengers died;

✈ in 9 per cent of accidents between 90 and 100 per cent of passengers died;

✈ in 27 per cent of accidents between 10 and 90 per cent of passengers died;

✈ in 23 per cent of accidents between 0 and 10 per cent of passengers died.

Therefore, in an aircraft accident involving fatalities you have about an even chance of survival.

Q HAS FLYING BECOME SAFER IN THE PAST 20 YEARS?

The rate of fatal accidents for passenger aircraft has not changed significantly over the past 15 years, but since the number of flights has more than doubled during that time, the number of fatal aircraft accidents has increased accordingly. This, together with the media coverage and understandable public concern, might lead you to assume that flying is less safe now than it was 20 years ago. This is not the case. However, it is disappointing that improvement in the technology of flying has not led to an increase in safety during this time.

▣ HOW CAN I OPTIMIZE MY SAFETY ON BOARD AN AIRCRAFT?

✈ Choose airlines of the major industrialized countries. These airlines are strictly regulated by their respective Civil Aviation Authorities, and so too is their air traffic control system. Also, choose airlines that have good time-performance statistics, low passenger-complaint levels and no financial problems. This information can generally be found in the media or on the internet.

✈ Choose larger aircraft. Aircraft with over 30 passenger seats are designed and certified to the strictest regulations and, in the event of an accident, provide a better chance for passenger survival.

✈ Fly non-stop routes. Most accidents occur during the take-off, the climb, the descent and the landing, so reducing the amount of flying cycles reduces risk.

✈ Pay attention to the flight safety briefing. Pay particular attention to the site of your nearest available emergency exit.

✈ Keep the overhead storage locker free of heavy articles. If you have trouble lifting an item into an overhead storage locker then it should not be there and could be a danger in severe turbulence.

✈ Keep your seat belt fastened while seated. This provides extra protection in the event of the aircraft encountering turbulence.

✈ Listen to the flight attendants; they are there, primarily, for your safety.

✈ Let the flight attendants pour your hot drinks; they are trained to do it.

✈ In the event of any emergency, stay calm, keep your wits about you and follow the directions of the flight attendants.

▣ WHAT TYPE OF EMERGENCY AM I MOST LIKELY TO FACE?

The two most common emergencies are an emergency evacuation using the slides, and a requirement to use the emergency oxygen supply in the event of a sudden cabin depressurization or if the cabin fills with smoke. In both cases it is more likely that the emergency will be declared as a precaution and you will not be in imminent danger.

◻ WHAT TYPE OF EMERGENCY AM I MOST LIKELY TO FACE? (CONTINUED)

Emergency evacuations
Be familiar with the nearest exit and remove high-heeled shoes that could tear the emergency slide.

Emergency oxygen
Your first priority is to put on your own mask before helping others. In a sudden cabin depressurization you risk losing consciousness. Only by helping yourself first will you be in a position to help children or other passengers with theirs.

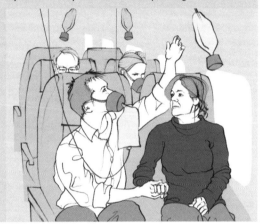

Always remember that despite some of the answers above, flying remains the safest form of modern travel, with less than one accident leading to at least one fatality per one million flights. When you are flying there will be about 13 million others like you, making, in total, over 15 billion passenger journeys per year around the world.

Your main concern should, therefore, be for your own health while on your flight, especially if you are a frequent long-haul business traveller. By now you should be more informed about your surroundings, both within and without the aircraft, and have a greater understanding of what is happening around you during the various phases of flight in a modern passenger aircraft. Follow the strategies for maintaining your own health and well being before, during and after a flight and you will be able to enjoy a safe, comfortable and healthy flight!

INDEX